BARRIER BREAKERS

BARRIER BREAKERS

Ignite Your Faith, Stir Your Spirit, and
Destroy the Works of the Devil Surrounding Your Life

Hank Kunneman

DESTINY IMAGE® PUBLISHERS, INC.

P.O. Box 310, Shippensburg, PA 17257-0310

"Speaking to the Purposes of God for This Generation and for the Generations to Come."

This book and all other Destiny Image, Revival Press, MercyPlace, Fresh Bread, Destiny Image Fiction, and Treasure House books are available at Christian bookstores and distributors worldwide.

For a U.S. bookstore nearest you, call **1-800-722-6774**.

For more information on foreign distributors, call **717-532-3040**.

Reach us on the Internet: **www.destinyimage.com**.

ISBN 13 TP: 978-0-7684-3227-5

ISBN 13 HC: 978-0-7684-3608-2

ISBN 13 LP: 978-0-7684-3609-9

ISBN 13 Ebook: 978-0-7684-9081-7

For Worldwide Distribution, Printed in the U.S.A.

2 3 4 5 6 7 / 14 13 12 11

DEDICATION

This book is dedicated to my two sons, Matthew and Jonathan, who are the continuing future of *Barrier Breakers!*

ENDORSEMENTS

Everyone needs breakthrough. When I read this book, I see the generational blessing of breakthrough. What a great revelation to work in your life on a daily basis as a born-again Christian. Read it and "break through."

—Dr. Marilyn Hickey
President, Marilyn Hickey Ministries

Hank Kunneman has been a guest on my television show, *It's Supernatural*. I am amazed at his accurate gift of prophecy that is well documented.

—Sid Roth
Host, *It's Supernatural*

This book is your ticket to deliverance from a myriad of personal challenges you face! Hank Kunneman helps us find the place of breakthrough with practical and inspirational guidance. This work looks at real people from the Bible and gives us prescriptions for victorious living. Hank Kunneman is emerging as one of the nation's most insightful, prophetic teachers. Read this book and thrive!

—Bishop Harry R. Jackson Jr.
Senior Pastor of Hope Christian Church Washington, DC
Founder and President High Impact Leadership Coalition

In the natural world, things often break down, but in the supernatural realm, there is always room for a breakthrough if we believe God and persevere with our faith. In this book, my good friend Hank opens the Word of God and shows the path to miracle breakthroughs you must have in whatever area in your life you must have it.

—Richard Roberts, B.A., M.A., D.Min.
Oral Roberts Ministries

We are in a time of urgency. Individuals, churches, and nations need a breakthrough. The forces of darkness appear to have the upper hand. *Barrier Breakers* is a timely reminder that the Lord is still on His throne!

This book in your hands is a provocation to find your breakthrough, but more than that, to be an agent of breakthrough in many lives and situations. *Barrier Breakers* is rooted in the Word of God demonstrating from many Scriptures God's eternal purpose for His people to live in the freedom of His victory. Read, enjoy, and be a *Barrier Breaker.*

—Alan and Eileen Vincent
Outpouring Ministries and City Reachers *for the Love of San Antonio*

Hank Kunneman has done it again! Another life-rescuing, powerful book to set your soul free. You will not be able to lay it down. It not only brings anointing to set you free and to heal you but also a power to break those barriers that have imprisoned you. What a book in such a day as this. Very timely, Hank, thanks.

—Mark T. Barclay Rev., PhD

If there is a word combination found in the history of Christian experience that exudes joy, excitement, and enthusiasm among believers it is the word *"breakthrough."* If there is anything desired in the Christian walk, or in the life of the prayer warrior, the pastor, teacher, prophet, apostle, evangelist, or lay person in the church, it is to see the breakthrough fought for, longed for, and expected. I heartily recommend this book to all those whose dreams have lingered for a long while, whose prayers seem to be up for grabs as to the outcome, and whose hearts have ached for the day of fulfillment of the promises of God. Get ready for your victory! Read this book in joy!

—Pastor Larry Gordon
Cornerstone World Outreach
Sioux City, IA

CONTENTS

FOREWORD

I have written many Forewords for different people, and it has always been a blessing and a privilege to do so. This time it is an especially joyous honor because Hank Kunneman, aside from being my best friend and a great prophet of God, is also a man known for his integrity, moral righteousness, and transparent family life.

I consider him to be greatly used by God in this generation—one of the most precise prophets in his office. I can testify to every prophetic word he has declared over my life, ministry, and family and of its fulfillment. His ministry is touching people in the United States and other nations around the world.

Barrier Breakers was inspired by God to bring a new revelation to many, especially to those passive believers who are still waiting for everything to be handed over to them. In this book, Hank Kunneman teaches us how to use the same principle by which Jesus destroyed the serpent. He gives clear instruction as to how to develop a spirit of warfare and experience breakthroughs in our lives. Furthermore, he gives us the keys needed to destroy financial, emotional, and other types of barriers; this information is greatly needed, especially at this time in which the world is experiencing difficult situations that affect believers and nonbelievers alike.

Finally, Pastor Hank teaches how we can successfully achieve breakthroughs by praying in the Spirit. Speaking in other tongues is a gift rarely practiced today, but Hank breaks this barrier by bringing forth the fresh and powerful revelation of praying in the Spirit as a weapon to defeat the enemy and his evildoings. This book reveals how to destroy the strongholds that keep churches and believers from moving in the fullness of their calling and how to cause powerful, positive changes in every area. I can faithfully testify of the breakthroughs I have personally experienced after knowing this truth about the Kingdom. This is a book for all pastors, leaders, and believers at every level.

—Guillermo Maldonado
Pastor of King Jesus International Ministry

INTRODUCTION

An offensive thrust that penetrates and carries beyond a defensive line in warfare or an act or instance of breaking through an obstacle; a sudden advance especially in knowledge or technique

After many years in the ministry, and pastoring a church, I have encountered many things in working with people and ministering into their lives. If there is something I have learned specifically, it is that there seems to be one key difference between those who succeed at life or in dealing with problems and those who don't. It's attitude. People who succeed simply won't take no for an answer to the problems and hindrances of life. They will keep chipping away at the issue at hand until they find their sense of resolve. In other words, they keep speaking to that pain in their body until it subsides. They will stay with God no matter the cost. They will work hard until they see the fruit of their labor. They will do everything it takes to get their promise from God.

This attitude is a breakthrough attitude, but as I looked at this more closely, I also realized something else about it. It isn't just an attitude you work hard to develop. It is something that every Christian was born into! It is like spiritual DNA. We actually have a spiritual imprint from God once we become born-again believers that enables us to break through.

I have found countless examples of this powerful truth woven all through the Bible. It all began, of course, in the Garden of Eden. Man fell, and the battle was on! We find that the devil was seeking to stop the human race that was created in God's own image. The devil thought he won the final victory the day man fell. God declared the ultimate blow against him by speaking a prophetic mystery of a deliverer who would crush the serpent, the devil, and redeem fallen man. What would follow changed history and eternity forever! Heaven and earth collided as God sent His own Son to fulfill this promise and be born into the world. For the most part we know the story, but some of the most powerful revelation that affects our lives is not only in the fact that Jesus came, but also in *how* He came. It had to do with the family line or seed from which Jesus would be born. Jesus wasn't born from just any family. He was born from a line of people handpicked by God because they all had one quality in common. They carried a breakthrough spirit. They weren't quitters, and they didn't take no for an answer.

This family line, which included people like Jacob, Pharez, David, and more, was able to carry the royal heritage of blessing that ultimately produced Jesus. We find that these had to overcome setback after setback and every imaginable attack of the devil, who was doing everything possible to destroy this royal seed. It was the seed that would produce the promised deliverer, the ultimate barrier breaker. We will even find how this same breakthrough quality existed in Joseph and Mary. God chose them because He knew they would protect the seed of breakthrough with their lives. They wouldn't allow anything to steal their promise.

Of course, these barrier breakers of the Bible were catalysts who brought the promised deliverer, Jesus, into the earth. Of course, the devil thought he had defeated Jesus and finally ended this line of barrier breakers by having Him crucified. With nails in His hands and feet, a sword thrust into His side, and a striking of His head and the plowing upon His back with whips, it appeared there would be no possible fulfilling of God's promise.

Yet with every strike from the enemy, something was being birthed. Had the enemy known what was about to happen through Jesus' crucifixion, he would not have crucified this royal seed. What he didn't know is that this spiritual DNA, which existed in the line of people who brought Jesus into the earth, was now going to continue in everyone thereafter who was born into Christ! What a blow to the devil! Jesus crushed the head of the serpent, and when you gave your life to Christ, that serpent-crushing ability was imparted into you. You are part of that same royal line of barrier breakers that has the ability to bring the seed of Christ into the earth. You are His powerful witness of the resurrection. The attitude needed for success isn't just something you have to try and create with your own willpower. It is something that is in you because you are born from barrier-breaking seed! It is in your spiritual DNA. Just like Jesus, and even the line of barrier breakers before Him, you can overcome fear, disease, torment, and yes, setback after setback! You can have this not only in your life, but you can also reproduce it again into the lives of others as you share the power of Christ with them. The line of barrier breakers didn't end with Jesus; it was just the beginning! Now multitudes and generations of those spiritually born of His Kingdom have arisen, and we carry His serpent-crushing DNA! A new generation of barrier breakers has been born.

May this book help you rise up and no longer tolerate what seems to resist, hinder, frustrate, or stand in your way! May it be a turning point that will teach you how to operate in what is already inside you so you can become a devil crusher just the way Jesus crushed the head of the serpent. Your faith will be ignited and your spirit stirred to get the results you have been praying for. Discover the process of how to operate in the spirit of breakthrough so you can see your victory through to completion, just the way Jesus and those of the royal seed were able to do. Once you step into it, you will begin to walk in breakthrough after breakthrough and watch yourself become a true *barrier breaker!*

Chapter One

THE SERPENT CRUSHER

And I will put enmity between thee and the woman, and between thy seed and her seed; it shall bruise thy head, and thou shalt bruise his heel (Genesis 3:15).

I could hardly believe my eyes! Did I just see what I thought I saw? I was mowing the lawn of our newly rented house located next to a quiet farm field. With my heart racing, I checked the surroundings of my yard, replaying in my mind what had just happened. I was sure I saw what looked like a snake slither past me as I was mowing. There it went again, and yes, it *was* a snake! To my dismay, I would soon find that this would not be a one-time occurrence but rather something I continued to contend with as long as we rented this home. The yard of our house was nearly infested with snakes, probably because of the adjacent field. They would slither into the garage, around the foundation, through the yard, and even on one occasion slithered through our front door!

Truthfully, like most people, I dread snakes. Every time I mowed the lawn or went behind the house or out to the shed, I would see them. I must have had the most crookedly mowed lawn because I would constantly be looking out for them while trying to mow a straight line. Of course, my wife, Brenda, will always say they were the size of her pinky finger, but I, on the other hand, will beg to differ. In my recollection, they were big and ugly enough to move the house a full city block should they slither under the foundation! In either case, whether her story or mine, we tolerated these snakes for the two years we lived there, even though we were kind of afraid of them. However, because they were so common, we didn't feel there was really anything we could do, and eventually we somehow got used to their presence.

I share this story because this is how many of us tolerate that old serpent—you know, the devil! Rather than resist him, bind him up, and cast him out, we tolerate him and are afraid to deal with him. Then we eventually get used to him and sometimes even explain him away with excuses like, "Well it really isn't a demon; it's just an emotional imbalance, and I will probably have it for the rest of my life!"

What we really need to acknowledge is that we need a breakthrough against the power of that snake! However, this is how many in need of a breakthrough approach life. They don't want to look for a way to overcome the problem; they learn to live life with the problem. Whether it is a breakthrough in finances, marriage, health, relationships, occupation, family, or just life itself, we allow situations like with the snakes in our yard to control our lives and dictate how we live. I was jumping around the yard mowing in a zigzag pattern instead of being able to confidently mow a straight line. We find ourselves adapting to the problem rather than being determined to get rid of it and persisting until we break through.

You see, I never got a breakthrough with those snakes and lived in constant complaining and fear because of them. These snakes weren't even the poisonous kind but rather just the old, ugly, harmless garter snakes. This alone points out another truth as to how we often approach life. We give things power to control our thoughts and actions when really they have no power over us except what we believe. While the snakes in my yard were harmless, I turned them into monsters in my own mind. Rather than find a way to address them and deal with them, I did everything I could to avoid them. Can you see that this is often how we deal with the devil or other issues?

We can't just learn to live with the devil and the intrusions he makes into our lives. The Bible calls him *"that old serpent"* (Rev. 12:9), and we can't be tricked into believing there is nothing we can do to deal with him and overcome his power. No, instead, we need to develop what I like to call a *barrier breaker spirit!*

What is that, you might say? A barrier breaker is a person who looks at problems, refuses to run from them, and finds every way possible to break through them.

The Serpent Crusher

As Christians, we need to be barrier breakers who live creating our own spiritual breakthroughs. We need to be serpent crushers! After all, this is what God said He would do to the devil after man had sinned. He would send Jesus to crush the devil's head, and the only thing the devil would do was bruise Jesus' heel in the process! God didn't tolerate the devil's intrusion when he tempted Adam and Eve. Instead He declared war on the devil and even prophesied that He would send a seed, the Messiah, to crush the devil's plans and retrieve His man back from satan's clutches. Look at Genesis 3:15 (NIV): *"And I will put enmity between you and the woman, and between your offspring and hers; he will crush your head, and you will strike his heel."*

Here is the part I want you to see. God's breakthrough didn't all happen in one miraculous moment. This is where many of us miss our breakthrough. We want something that just jumps on us in one moment, while we lay back in the hammock drinking iced tea! We think the snakes are going to miraculously disappear on their own while we calmly think happy thoughts.

No, God's breakthrough to crush the serpent started with nothing more than a tiny seed! Oh the power of a seed! When God mentioned the seed of the woman, little did the devil know that God was prophesying a mystery about a future barrier breaker who would come to bring breakthrough for His people! This breaker would be the Messiah, the Savior of the world. This reveals just how much God loves you and me. It also shows how determined the Lord is about our lives and how much He doesn't tolerate the devil concerning us. God declared war after man sinned. He was declaring that a breaker was coming who would crush the devil's head! I like how The Message Bible says it regarding how God dealt with the devil!

God told the serpent: "Because you've done this, you're cursed, cursed beyond all cattle and wild animals, cursed to slink on your belly and eat dirt all your life. I'm declaring war between you and the Woman, between your off-spring and hers. He'll wound your head, you'll wound his heel" (Genesis 3:14-15 MSG).

God was declaring that there would be enmity, war, or hostility that would come between God and the devil, and the seed of woman would be used to destroy the seed of the devil. In this prophetic declaration, He showed us a powerful principle we can also use to break through any barriers in our lives. We can see from this prophecy the powerful principle of seeds and how God used them to crush the serpent. Your breakthrough today begins with a seed.

First, however, you and I have to realize that just as Jesus was a serpent crusher, so are we called to crush the power of the devil. The Bible tells us that the God of peace has crushed satan beneath our feet. Romans 16:20 says:

The God of peace will soon crush Satan under your feet. The grace of our Lord Jesus be with you (NIV).

That makes you a serpent crusher. You don't have to avoid and run from the devil. You, like God, have been given the power to overcome him. It is not based on how you feel or the difficulties and challenges you are facing. You have been made to be a serpent crusher through the Lord Jesus Christ, and we will see later how His seed was literally imparted into your spiritual DNA, making you a serpent crusher too! The seed of Christ in you has given you that power. Luke 10:19 says:

Behold, I give unto you power to tread on serpents and scorpions, and over all the power of the enemy: and nothing shall by any means hurt you.

In this life, there will always be obstacles that are in the path of our break-through. Many in this world today are facing difficult times and desperately need that breakthrough. What often happens is that many believers don't understand how to cultivate breakthrough that begins with a seed and grows into a miracle. A breakthrough spirit must be developed; it can't just be hoped for or waited for. We need to think of breakthrough like growing up from an embryo in our mother's womb to childhood and on to full mature adulthood. It's a process, and the seed of Christ has already been placed inside you! However, we need to take our rightful place and determine to be a barrier breaker with that seed. It requires work and our obedience.

Some will think that is too hard because breakthrough unfortunately has become a cliché and has lost some of its real purpose and meaning. Often many who speak of it only do so in the excitement of the moment at church and often they expect some quick fix. Breakthrough is a process, and as you progress through the pages of this book, you will gain the necessary understanding of how to obtain a breakthrough. It is important to understand that in the process of breakthrough, as in everything in life and creation, there must always be a seed in its beginning. The seed is the beginning element that you need to bring forth your blessing. A seed was provided for you and me in the person of Jesus! He crushed and defeated the devil on our behalf and put that seed into us.

The Mystery of the Barrier Breaker

There is a powerful mystery that the Bible speaks of regarding seeds. We can see this truth even in the opening Scripture that we learned of the seed of the Messiah in Jesus Christ. Inside this seed mystery is the power to be a barrier breaker and to receive a breakthrough. Our seed is of the incorruptible seed of Christ. However, the devil tries to sow other "weed" seeds. We just have to decide which seeds we want to cultivate—Christ's seed in us or the devil's intrusive seeds. Seeds are cultivated by choices, actions, and thoughts. In Christianity, we often think of seeds as our financial giving or our offerings since so much preaching has surrounded that aspect of seeds. That is true—financial giving can act like seeds that grow into a harvest. However, the seed mystery overall in Scripture is the seed that begins in your heart that you cultivate over time in your life.

First, let's look at the mystery surrounding the seed of Jesus Christ found in the Bible. It will give us a basic insight into how spiritual seeds work.

A seed would arise to crush the devil's head. We know this seed was the Messiah and every Christian that would be born of Him or again by Him (see Gen. 3:15). Spiritual seeds have the power to defeat the powers of darkness.

This seed of Christ had to die.

> *I tell you the truth, unless a kernel of wheat falls to the ground and dies, it remains only a single seed. But if it dies, it produces many seeds* (John 12:24 NIV).

The grain of wheat Christ was speaking of was His life. His life was the seed of Genesis 3:15 that would die for all humankind. When He died as the seed on the cross, He would reproduce more seeds through His resurrection. Those seeds are you and me! Think of it like an ear of corn. You plant one kernel into the ground, and essentially that kernel in its current state dies. However, afterward it resurrects into a new identity and reproduces many new kernels of corn, or many new seeds. Seeds die, resurrect, and then produce a harvest.

Christ was the mysterious seed that fooled the devil, as it says in First Corinthians 2:7-8:

> *But we speak the wisdom of God in a mystery, even the hidden wisdom, which God ordained before the world unto our glory: which none of the princes of this world knew: for had they known it, they would not have crucified the Lord of glory.*

This verse tells us that if the devil would have known this mystery, he and his demons would never have crucified the Lord of glory! The devil knew a serpent crusher had been prophesied, but he had no idea that he was coming in the form of incorruptible seed. You cannot kill incorruptible seed because it carries the power to resurrect and reproduce! Satan failed to understand that by killing Jesus, the incorruptible seed of Christ was going to reproduce many sons unto glory who carry that same incorruptible seed. He thought Jesus was like everyone else, of corruptible human seed, making Him subject to the power of death. The devil and all the hordes of hell didn't fully understand the mystery of Christ being born of incorruptible seed. Seeds can produce a harvest even when it looks like nothing is happening!

Many Christians fail to understand the power in a seed for breakthrough and blessing. They often can't see past the troubles of today because they don't realize the power of incorruptible seed within them that can produce a breakthrough. It gives us some insight as to why Jesus was able to see past the pain of the cross. Hebrews 12:2 says, *". . .who for the joy that was set before Him endured the cross, despising the shame and is set down at the right hand of the throne of God."*

Jesus knew what happens when seeds die in the ground. Because He was born of a virgin, He didn't carry the seed of corruption and death that was passed to all men through Adam's sin (see Rom. 5:18). He was born of seed that cannot be held by death. Therefore, He knew it was vital for Him to die on the cross, because if there was no seed planted through His death, then there would be no breakthrough of resurrection and as a result no other seeds reproduced. That is why He looked past the pain of the cross. He knew that the seed He was about to plant of His own life was going to destroy the devil and that same incorruptible seed would now be passed down into every person who trusts in the name of Jesus Christ.

I can only imagine what the devil must have thought when Jesus arose from the grave and all the demonic powers realized that not only could they *not* kill the seed of Christ, but that they enabled many others to be born of that same incorruptible power! The devil just didn't bank on the fact that Jesus was a seed that was going to reproduce many more just like Him who have the power to crush the serpent.

Look at John 12:24 (NIV): *"But if it dies, it produces many seeds."* This is because everything reproduces after its kind, or the way it was created (see Gen. 1:11-12). If Christ is a seed, then what did He produce when He was "planted" or died? The answer is you and me, and we carry His serpent-crushing DNA! Look also at Romans 6:5, which says, *"For if we have been planted together in the likeness of His death, we shall be also in the likeness of His resurrection."* Another verse, First John 4:17, reveals this same truth of who we are, Christians walking as He did in the earth. It says:

Herein is our love made perfect, that we may have boldness in the day of judgment: because as He is, so are we in this world.

Review again the process in Scripture:

- A seed is promised to come and crush the devil and redeem man (see Gen. 3:15).
- This seed has to die so it can produce more seeds (Christians) (see John 12:24).

We are planted with Christ in His death and resurrection (see Rom. 6:5).

If the devil knew the mystery in Christ, he wouldn't have crucified the Lord (see 1 Cor. 2:7-8).

Every seed produces after its kind (see Gen. 1:11-12).

So the result was others just like Him in the earth walking in the same power as He did (see 1 John 2:17).

One of the most incredible revelations we can have is to understand the mystery of Christ, the barrier-breaking seed. That is because we then understand how much like Christ we really are! To the devil in the earth we look like Jesus! We have His authority and His power to destroy the powers of darkness. Think about what Jesus said in John 14:12, when He said, *"He that believeth on Me, the works that I do shall he do also; and greater works than these shall he do; because I go unto My Father."* The power Jesus walked in lives and operates in you! Just like tomato seeds produce more tomatoes, Jesus dying as the seed produces more seeds just like Him! This is why Jesus referred to Himself as the vine and to us as the branches, meaning that we are from the same seed that has grown into one unified plant!

Oh, I know the devil regrets the day he crucified Jesus!

We are in the same image as Jesus, and we too have a breakthrough, serpent-crushing spirit. In fact, we were born naturally and spiritually from a winning seed! Think about it—when millions of sperm cells from your father entered your mother, these cells rushed toward the egg inside her. However, only one sperm cell was able to enter the egg and conceive you. The one that entered was the winner! It won over millions of others. Even the process of conception sets you up as a winner. You were born from winning seed! There are no born losers. Whether born naturally or again spiritually through Jesus, we were all born to win through a seed.

Your conception and your very beginning set you up for breakthrough. The same is true for you when you were born again. You were born again from winning seed, and that is from the barrier-breaking seed of Jesus Christ.

War Over the Breakthrough Seed

It is because of the mystery that was in the seed of Christ and what His death and resurrection produced that the devil trembles. He continues to try every way possible to interfere and stop the Lord and His Church. Because of the mystery in Christ, it produced more just like Him called Christians, walking in the same power. This is why there has always been a war over the seed of man. The devil fears the power of what a seed can produce. He fears it so much, in fact, that this is why the Scripture says the devil comes immediately to steal the seed sown. Scripture says this seed is the word of God, which is also Christ. When Christ is sown in your heart when you believe in Him, He produces life. In the same way, since Jesus Christ and His Word are one in the same (see John 1:1), when you hear His Words and they are sown into your heart, they produce life. Look at Mark 4:15 (MSG):

> *The farmer plants the Word. Some people are like the seed that falls on the hardened soil of the road. No sooner do they hear the Word than Satan snatches away what has been planted in them.*

The devil doesn't want those seeds of God's Word to grow in your heart, so he tries to abort them as soon as you hear them. He brings other interferences, distractions, and counter ideas. This is also why the devil promotes and is the root source of abortion. This is because he is out to destroy the seed of man. If you have ever seen an aborted fetus, it is horrible, deplorable, and it is not difficult to see that this is the work of darkness and not the loving heart of our heavenly Father. Abortion is murder, and the devil is behind it, because he is the destroyer of seeds.

Jesus told us in Scripture that satan is a murderer and the father of all lies (see John 8:44). That is because satan is after the incorruptible seed of God that works in the hearts of men. He attempts to kill it through the use of deception and lies. We can see this further in Revelation 12:17, which says:

> And the dragon was wroth with the woman, and went to make war with the remnant of her seed, which keep the commandments of God, and have the testimony of Jesus Christ.

Ever since the day that God declared war on the devil in Genesis 3:15, satan has been trying to fight back. He was looking to destroy the coming barrier breaker before his head would be crushed. However, even though Jesus defeated him, satan is still at war with the incorruptible seed. All the way from Genesis to Revelation the serpent, which eventually is seen as a dragon by the end of the Bible, is still trying to destroy every seed of God's Word that he can find. He looks for every person who carries this seed and tries to steal from him or her, kill him or her, and destroy him or her (see John 10:10).

This is why when Moses was a small child, satan stirred up Pharaoh to have the male children murdered when they were born. Exodus 1:22 says:

> And Pharaoh charged all his people, saying, Every son that is born ye shall cast into the river, and every daughter ye shall save alive.

Again, satan was after that seed.

The devil did a similar thing during the time that Jesus was born and grew to a small child. He tried to kill the seed again by having the children murdered under two years of age (see Matt. 2:16). Again, this is why the devil loves the smell of the blood from aborted babies; he hates any possibility of another human being having the ability to carry the seed of God's Word in them. It is a satisfaction to him that he has destroyed another seed that could arise to crush his head again in the earth in the name of the Lord most High! You see, Moses was *a* seed, Jesus was *"the"* seed, and you are Christ's seed according to the promise if you are born again! Pharaoh and Herod were after the children, because they were motivated by the devil who remembered there was a prophecy by God in Genesis 3:15. This promise declared a bringing of a breakthrough for man and a crushing to the devil through a seed. Now, you as a Christian are the seed of Christ that the devil fears because of the harvest of what you will bring to honor and glorify God! First Peter 1:23 says, *"Being born again, not of corruptible seed, but of incorruptible, by the word of God, which liveth and abideth for ever."*

Never forget that you were born for a purpose! Your life is not meant for struggle after struggle or one frustration after another. Jesus wants you as a Christian to live a blessed life and to have it more abundantly. This doesn't mean you will never struggle or have difficult situations to face. What it means is that you carry the ability to overcome these struggles through the break-through seed within you. Even Jesus said in this life we would at times have tribulation (see John 16:33). That is because satan will continue to war for the incorruptible seed of God that has the potential to work in every human heart that comes to Christ. So he attempts to destroy and interfere in the lives of every human being alive to prevent it from happening.

What we have to realize is that we can win that war because of the power of God available to us when we received Christ's incorruptible seed. It is first the seed of your life, and then it is to be followed by seeds of choices, actions, giving, serving, and seeking the Lord. We must never forget that we are meant and purposed by God to bring forth a fruitful harvest from these seeds, which brings glory to Him. We are in a war fighting for the power of the seed of God! We can't give up, because if we do we will miss out on the blessing the seed in our hearts has the power to produce.

This war over the seed reminds me of a couple gardening stories when I was I growing up. When I was just a young boy, my father decided to plant a very large garden in our backyard. It was big enough to provide vegetables for the whole family. I came from a family of nine, including my mother and father, so having this garden produce would have been a great blessing.

One day, after the garden had started producing its crops, my dad asked my brother and me to get rid of the unwanted weeds that had been growing. Dad explained the difference between the weeds and plants and told us to pick each weed by hand. However, as kids do, we probably didn't listen as closely as we should have. All we could think of was how much dreaded work it was going to be, and the garden was huge! There were weeds everywhere.

Now, it was summer and we wanted to go swimming rather than spend the entire day working in the yard. Although instructed by Dad to pull the weeds by hand, we decided to use a garden hoe, thinking it would save time so we could go swimming. Of course, in addition, we weren't listening when Dad showed us how to recognize a weed, so now armed with the wrong tool and our own ignorance, we started chopping at would-be weeds. This led to a pretty big "war over the seeds" between my brother and me. We got into a big argument and started using the garden tools as weapons against each other and the plants all because we wanted to go swimming. By the time it was over, we had hoed down most everything growing in the garden. We both looked at the garden, which almost no longer existed because it had been attacked and hoed to death by our tools of anger! As you can imagine, my brother and I got in *Big* trouble with a capital B!

Our war-like fight led to a destroying of the harvest of vegetables and all the hard work that went into producing it. We allowed our arguing, fighting, disobedience, and our sloppy, lazy, uncaring attitude to destroy the blessing that could have not only benefited us but our entire family.

This is exactly what the devil intends for the seed of our lives and the seeds of what we want to produce. He wants to absolutely destroy us and our harvest so we look on life with frustration, regrets, and even severe consequences at times. This is so we don't receive breakthrough blessings in either our lives or for the lives of others.

After our garden war, it didn't make matters any better that my brother and I tried to repair it by replanting the hoed-down weeds and plants! Of course, they wouldn't grow again because they lost their roots and were completely destroyed, plus the soil was in pretty bad shape. As punishment, my brother and I had to can tomatoes with our parents and grandparents for an entire day. It was miserable. It smelled so bad, and we had to wait for those silly jars to pop indicating they were sealed. Worse yet, all the kids in the neighborhood teased us as we listened to them playing football while we were canning!

This garden story depicts how the devil wars for our seeds. However, here is what he does. He will do to us exactly what happened with my brother and me. He will trick you into destroying it yourself. He will deceive you into thinking that cultivating the seed is too much work or that there are just better ways to spend your time. The devil will try to get you to make the soil of your heart unreceptive to the incorruptible seed through things like hurt feelings, resentment, or bitterness. He will try to confuse you into what a "weed" really looks like, so you end up mistaking it for a plant. That is because he is a liar, but if we keep our eyes on the Word and on the seed of God in our hearts, we will continue to break through until the harvest of blessing comes!

Breakthrough Soil

The Lord tells us a story in Mark 4 concerning a sower who sowed seeds into different kinds and conditions of soil. There have been many great sermons preached from this passage of Scripture. The seeds Jesus was referring to were Kingdom seeds of the Word of God, but the important lesson Jesus draws out is that these seeds need the right soil or foundation to survive and bring forth a breakthrough blessing in our lives. The interesting thing that must not be overlooked is that Jesus talked about things that attack these seeds that are sown. He instructed us of things that will affect our lives and likened our spiritual foundation and heart to that of being like soil (see Mark 4). It is often these things that keep us from being barrier breakers or keep our breakthroughs from coming. Notice the different things that come to affect the soil of our lives, our hearts, and spiritual foundations we build on.

Mark 4:14-18

1. *The devil:* "...*Satan cometh immediately, and taketh away the word that was sown in their hearts*" (Mark 4:15). When we refuse to deal with the devil and demonic strongholds and refuse to close

the door to him in our lives, we will not be successful barrier breakers! He comes after the seeds of God in our lives so we won't have breakthrough.

2. *Out-of-control emotions and those who don't govern their souls.*

> *And these are they likewise which are sown on stony ground; who, when they have heard the word, immediately receive it with gladness; and have no root in themselves, and so endure but for a time: afterward, when affliction or persecution ariseth for the word's sake, immediately they are offended* (Mark. 4:16-17).

There are many who are like these seeds that fell on stony ground. Their Christian walk and foundation is like this soil. It is rocky, stony at best. The seed of their Christian life produces little to no fruit because they live for the moment. If life is good and things are going well, then they are happy, but as soon as things go wrong, they become an emotional wreck. They don't break through in their spirit but rather live according to how they feel at the moment. You see, your soul is your mind, will, and emotions. According to Jesus, we are to possess our soul (see Luke 21:19).

In order to possess our soul, we have to put reigns on it like we do when we ride a horse. If the horse starts going too fast and is getting out of control or going the wrong way, we pull back on the reigns to redirect the horse by saying, "Whoa!" This is exactly how we need to reign in our emotions so we can get a breakthrough. We must steer emotions toward the Word and spiritual things and not let it get out of control!

3. *Cares of this world, fear, anxiety, carnality and casual Christianity.*

> *And the cares of this world, and the deceitfulness of riches, and the lusts of other things entering in, choke the word, and it becometh unfruitful* (Mark 4:19).

Some Christians never experience breakthrough because they are too easily distracted. They get caught up with chores, excess work, and the need to make money. They go overboard trying to live the American dream. Some are just too hungry for what the world has to offer. Thus these desires and distractions keep the seeds of God from ever growing to maturity where they can become a blessing.

4.   *The good soil is those who hear God's Word and do it.* These are the ones who build a solid spiritual Christian life. They seek the Lord and His Kingdom first and strive to build a godly, solid, biblical foundation based on the Word of God as their standard. They don't give up based on how they feel or because of worldly distractions. They stay the course until the harvest comes.

We can see from these verses in Mark 4 that Jesus was showing us how important it is, for those who want to be barrier breakers, to understand the power that is in a seed when it is sown. It is not just what is in a seed alone. He was also showing the significance of the heart and the soil of our spiritual foundation, which helps the seed to grow and to bring forth a life that bears good fruit. Every seed must have good soil or the right foundation. When this happens, the seed breaks through the surface of the soil from the right foundation and produces a harvest.

Jesus taught about the right foundations in Matthew 7 and Luke 6. He talks about how vital it is that our house, or our life, is built and established upon the right setting. He said storms will come in life and explained there are those who build wisely in life because they build their spiritual foundation on a rock or the right foundation because they hear and do the Word of God. He then taught about those who are foolish when the storms of life come because they build upon sand, which is not dependable or solid. He said great is the fall of those who build in this manner because they hear the words of God but don't do them. In other words, they don't grow their garden in the right stable environment, which is simply that they are consistent to do God's Word.

In this story, Jesus was teaching us how to get a breakthrough in our lives and be properly prepared for the trials and issues of life. Have you ever watched the weather report on television when they are reporting a hurricane? I am amazed and amused by these reporters who can stand there doing their job while a major hurricane is blowing through the city. Debris is falling and flying everywhere around the reporter as they duck to get out of the way and are barely able to stand. Yet, they still manage to stand with their hair and clothing askew giving the report. The officials tell everyone to evacuate, but somehow this must not apply to the reporters! It's hilarious!

Anyway, imagine how foolish it would be to see people trying to board up their windows under these conditions because they weren't fully prepared in advance. If you saw them trying to hammer up boards while the rain and wind were raging, you would assume they were crazy. However, this is how many approach life, and then they get frustrated when they don't get victory or break through. Instead, they are overcome by the storms of life. It doesn't have to be this way. The time to prepare is not when it is stormy, but before the storm comes. In advance, you fill yourself with the Word of God and spend time in prayer. It will set you on the right foundation, but actually something more takes place. As God's Word goes into your heart, not only is it preparing your foundational defenses against the devil, but God's Word is also the seed. This seed is entering the soil of your heart to produce provision for whatever you need when the storm hits!

Jesus taught this breakthrough principle throughout His teachings. Notice what He says in Luke 6:46-49:

> *And why call ye Me, "Lord, Lord," and do not the things which I say? Whosoever cometh to Me, and heareth My sayings, and doeth them, I will show you to whom he is like: He is like a man which built a house, and digged deep, and laid the foundation on a rock: and when the flood arose, the stream beat vehemently upon that house, and could not shake it: for it was founded upon a rock. But he that heareth, and doeth not, is like a man that without a foundation built an house upon the earth; against which the stream did beat vehemently, and immediately it fell; and the ruin of that house was great.*

In this passage, the Lord shows us how to prepare for challenges so we can not only be left standing but also so we can come out on top in full blessing and provision afterward. Jesus indicates several types of seeds we can sow that produce the harvest of blessing, but these same seeds also set us on the right foundation where the harvest of blessing is able to grow even when storms come. Let's look at the seeds we need to sow from the verses from Luke.

1. *Making Jesus truly Lord and doing what He says* (see Luke 6:46). If He is our Lord, then we need to do what He has said. If Jesus has told us that we should love, forgive, give offerings, serve, pray, and walk in righteousness (to name a few), then we should do it.

2. *Hearing His Word, and doing it* (see verse 47). This is whether it is His words in Scripture or His words by His Spirit spoken through the many different ways that God communicates.

3. *Digging deeper* (see verse 48). Digging deeper requires us to strive for more of God and being determined to make Him a priority and the key focus of our lives. This is making spiritual things a priority and being determined to daily pursue more of God and His Word. If we are not doing this, then we are just maintaining and won't have a strong spiritual foundation on which to stand or break through.

4. *Lay a foundation* (see verse 48). Laying a foundation is to daily go back to the simple things, the basics of your Christianity, and the Word of God. Strengthening and laying our spiritual foundations must be a continuous process. This makes our spiritual house stronger and durable to the storms and challenges of this life. When you rehearse and know the basics, it helps to repair or eliminate dangerous cracks in your spiritual foundation of life and avoid defeat. Like a good coach would say, know your playbook! In the same way, we need to know our Bibles as the basic foundation to our Christianity. Remember, Third John 2 shows us three primary things that will affect all men born in this world. Everybody deals with them. They are finances, health, and a healthy soul (mind, will, and emotions). Third John 1:2 says:

"Beloved, I wish above all things that thou mayest prosper and be in health, even as thy soul prospereth."

The second thing that was part of the process for a harvest and breakthrough was the foundation or the soil, as we mentioned earlier in Mark 4. Jesus said there were two foundations. The one established upon a rock will stand, and the other built on earth or sand will fall. It is those who submit to His Lordship, His Word, and are committed to digging deeper in the things of God and laying a sure foundation upon Him, who will be the most solid type of believers.

When I was in grade school, my dad decided to add on to our garage. In order to construct this new building, we had to dig deep into the ground to lay the right foundation to build and support the structure. It seemed that we dug so deep we were about to break through to the other side of the world! As a young kid, I kept expecting to hear voices from the other side of the world since we were digging so deep and someone had told me that China was on the other side. We had to dig deep enough that the structure could endure the different storms and adversities that might arise. There is no difference concerning our spiritual foundation and its importance to maintaining and receiving our breakthroughs in life. It is like Jesus said, those who dig deeper and seek to build upon a rock on a sure foundation are the ones who are wise and endure life's storms and challenges.

Sowing Seeds for Breakthrough

In this chapter we have learned that two basic things are needed for spiritual breakthrough and a life full of fruitful blessings. We have learned about the power of seeds and our need to continually sow the right ones, and we have also discussed the importance of having the right foundation. The right spiritual seeds and a solid foundation are vital for breakthrough. The seed and the soil, so simple!

This reminds me of another garden story. Of course, we didn't have just one! Once again my dad had asked one of my brothers and me to help plant a garden, and my grandpa, who was quite the gardener, was going to show us how. Grandpa started by explaining each packet of seeds to us and how to plant them. It seemed to take *forever* for him to explain. We were bored out of our minds and once again paid little to no attention and forgot everything we were told. This led to a pretty serious garden brawl between my brother and me after our grandpa left. We fought in that garden; punching, kicking, and wrestling on top of the dirt and the newly planted seeds! Of course, you would think no adult would ever leave us alone in the garden again, but I guess they still believed in us!

You can imagine how we ruined the garden of what we had planted. We were supposed to plant the seeds in rows, one kind of seed per row, and write the name of the seeds on a popsicle stick. We were then to put the sticks next to the correct row of seeds. Very simple, a carrot seed row needed the stick that said "carrots" to be put next to it. Right! Except for one problem! We were so busy fighting again that we messed up the sticks and rows of seeds and couldn't figure out what kinds of seeds were planted in which row! What a garden mess! My brother and I tried to cover our mess by guessing which stick should go next to each row. We then proceeded to put them next to the different rows of this very large garden, hoping we were right since we had no clue as to what was planted.

You know we found that it didn't matter what was written on the stick. The seeds that were planted in the garden soil still produced after their kind. A carrot seed produces carrots, not tomatoes. That's because, as we read before, every seed produces after its kind. It didn't matter what we wrote on the stick and placed incorrectly next to the seeds planted in the garden. The seeds themselves produced as they were created to and not according to how we labeled them.

The same principle is true when we sow spiritual seeds. In life, we reap what we sow. It doesn't matter what you label it or what you want to come up; we reap what we sow. The power of a seed is so powerful to get a breakthrough. If we sow the right seeds in life, we *will* get a breakthrough because we are cultivating the seed of Christ that is already in us. It has to take place because of a spiritual law. Give and it will be given back. Sow love and you will reap eventually. On the other hand, if you sow bitterness and hurt, you will reap those things. Just like the natural law of sowing corn seed gives you a harvest of corn, the spiritual law of sowing seeds works the same way!

Giving Your Maximum Best for Maximum Breakthrough

If we want a life of breakthrough and want to be a true barrier breaker, then we have to give God our best. We have to continue to prepare our hearts and lives as the soil if we want breakthrough to manifest. When we understand how powerful the seed of Jesus Christ was to break through against the devil's lies and wicked schemes, we will truly experience the breakthroughs we are expecting. We can't expect to have breakthrough if our hearts aren't right or our spiritual foundations are weak. We can't expect abundant breakthrough either if we are selfish, self-focused, and just give up in life. If we want maximum breakthrough, then we need to give maximum seeds of blessings to God and others.

In Luke 5 we see an example of how Jesus was trying to teach Peter how to get a breakthrough of maximum results. In this setting, Jesus was also in the process of choosing His twelve disciples and Peter would later be one of the main leaders of the Church after Jesus' resurrection. Peter needed to be transformed from Simon, which means, "a reed bending in the direction of the wind," into Peter, which means, "an unmovable rock." When Jesus met up with him here, He began the process by teaching Peter a principle about breakthrough. Jesus was transforming him into a barrier breaker who would know how to yield maximum results.

> And it came to pass, that, as the people pressed upon Him to hear the word of God, He stood by the lake of Gennesaret, and saw two ships standing by the lake: but the fishermen were gone out of them, and were washing their nets. And He entered into one of the ships, which was Simon's, and prayed him that he would thrust out a little from the land. And He sat down, and taught the people out of the ship. Now when He had left speaking, He said unto Simon, Launch out into the deep, and let down your nets for a draught.

And Simon answering said unto Him, Master, we have toiled all the night, and have taken nothing: nevertheless at thy word I will let down the net. And when they had this done, they inclosed a great multitude of fishes: and their net brake (Luke 5:1-6).

Typically when we read this story, we always think of the abundance of fish that came from the net. However, did Peter really get maximum results? Let's examine it for a moment. First, Peter had been fishing all night with his partners with no results. He had no breakthrough after a night of fishing and caught nothing.

Maybe you feel the same way as Peter. Perhaps you have been working hard at life, but feel you have had little to no results. However, there is a hidden key in this story that created Peter's breakthrough that is also a key for you too! Again, we will see the revelation of planting a seed as we have learned through this chapter. Remember, there is power in a seed. This is why Jesus said the mustard seed is the smallest of all seeds yet when it grows it becomes greater than all other plants. Why is this so? It is because of the power a seed possesses to bring breakthrough.

The same principle was the key to breakthrough for Peter, if he would only have realized it. Jesus knew this powerful seed principle. He knew that in order for Peter to get a breakthrough, a seed would be needed. Jesus had to get Peter to offer a seed, so He makes a request and asks him to launch out in the boat. The first seed that Jesus got Peter to offer was his ship: *"And He entered into one of the ships, which was Simon's, and prayed him that he would thrust out a little from the land"* (Luke 5:3).

If Peter would offer his ship, it would then be the necessary seed and foundation in which a breakthrough could be born and later brought into manifestation. When Jesus requested for Peter to launch out for a catch, Peter gave a seed of obedience. The seed of his boat was given at the request of the Master.

Peter "giving" his boat in an act of obedience caused the boat to become a seed. After all, this ship was Peter's livelihood, and I imagine after a long night it felt sacrificial to launch back out again! Don't be surprised if the Master comes for your livelihood as well and requires you to give a sacrificial seed in obedience to Him.

Peter's boat might have been the first seed, but if Peter was going to have maximum results, he would need more seed! So Jesus makes another request. This time Jesus asks him to let down his nets, plural, not singular for a catch of fish: *"Now when He had left speaking, He said unto Simon, Launch out into the deep, and let down your nets for a draught"* (Luke 5:4). Notice, Jesus said nets! It was to get Peter to sow seeds for a maximum breakthrough! There was only one problem in this yet to be a barrier breaker named Peter. He wasn't thinking about breakthrough or that there was any possibility of one. He was limiting Jesus by his own efforts and the daily routine of how life works. You work all day and night. Some days you catch a break and other days you don't. A different mind-set would be needed for Peter to become a barrier breaker.

Realize that when Jesus showed up, Peter and the rest of the crew were washing their nets they had been using to fish all that night. *"...But the fishermen were gone out of them, and were washing their nets"* (Luke 5:2). Fishing and cleaning nets is no easy task. But now, after the trouble of launching back out to sea, Jesus told Peter to let down his nets for a catch. Jesus said "nets" plural, but Peter did what many of us do. He said, "at your word I will let down the net," singular. *"And Simon answering said unto Him, Master, we have toiled all the night, and have taken nothing: nevertheless at Thy word I will let down the net"* (Luke 5:5).

In order to get maximum breakthrough, we need to have maximum obedience, even when it's tiring and feels like a whole lot of trouble! Jesus said nets, not net. He was asking for Peter's best!

However, Peter only let down one net. I mean, he was already washing the other nets; they were out where they could have easily been used again. Why couldn't he have just thrown them all back in the water? It makes me think that the net Peter was offering was perhaps a net that was a spare, maybe an old worn out one that was lying around, so he wouldn't have to dirty the other nets he just washed. It makes sense that maybe the one net he offered was an old spare because in other accounts of a supernatural catch of fish there is never any mention of the nets breaking, but in this account the net broke. John 21:11 says:

> *Simon Peter went up, and drew the net to land full of great fishes, an hundred and fifty and three: and for all there were so many,* **yet was not the net broken.**

Peter did what many of us do when we are wanting a breakthrough but don't think it will work. This mind-set keeps us from becoming a barrier breaker! So we pray half-hearted prayers. We hope and pray it might work this time, so we don't offer our best, like with Peter. Sometimes we refuse to offer our ship, or refuse to give God our best. Other times we spend all our time focusing, like Peter, on what we don't have and how hard we have been working, praying, and serving the Lord but haven't "caught" a break in a while! The end result is we never get the maximum blessing of breakthrough!

In conclusion, we can see the importance of Peter offering his ship that became the foundation and seed for his breakthrough. Had he not at least offered that much he would have received nothing. It was this decision that resulted in his net breaking, and he got the breakthrough because of a seed! However, if Peter would have had a barrier-breaking spirit and mind-set, he would have received a better end result. He would have stretched himself further for maximum results. Sure, he received a blessing, but how much more would he have received had he had a barrier-breaker spirit that was willing to work for a maximum result? All he had to do was what Jesus told him, and that was let down nets, not just *a* net!

> *And when they had this done, they inclosed a great multitude of fishes: and their net brake. And they beckoned unto their partners, which were in the other ship, that they should come and help them. And they came, and filled both the ships, so that they began to sink* (Luke 5:6-7).

After this happened, Peter knew he hadn't given Jesus his maximum best of giving his best nets as a seed. We know this by his response to Jesus. Luke 5:8

says, *"When Simon Peter saw it, he fell down at Jesus' knees, saying, Depart from me; for I am a sinful man, O Lord."*

Notice Peter admitted that he was a sinner, or he had sinned. Why would he say that if he gave his best? Again, giving Jesus our best will produce the best results!

Years ago, our whole family kept getting sick with little nagging illnesses like colds or the flu. One would get it, then another. Finally, after months of these cycles, we were all sick again and decided we'd had enough. I asked the Lord what we should do, and He told me to write out a check and give the money to a healing ministry. Right in the middle of the night after our son was up vomiting, we wrote the check. We didn't have much money, but nevertheless, we gave our very best. We sowed our best financial seed and planted it in a respected healing ministry. That powerful seed coupled with our obedience brought our breakthrough moment. Almost immediately, after we put the money in the mailbox, that assignment of the devil broke over our lives. We got a breakthrough from giving a seed, and we did it by giving our best seed.

Remember, there is power to break through in a seed! It can be seeds of our choices, actions, thoughts, and even financial giving. Now, rise up on the inside and know that the greater one lives within you, and because He was resurrected, you now possess the same power He had to be a barrier breaker. It is time for you to realize you possess the barrier-breaking spirit of Jesus Christ because His incorruptible seed lives in you. Keep your foundation strong in His Word, and continue to give your life as He gave His. Watch the seeds of your life and the choices you make, and the things you give for His honor, produce breakthrough after breakthrough for you! You are a barrier breaker created to continue to crush satan under your feet! Keep planting your seeds in life and continue to understand who you are and who lives in you and expect breakthrough upon breakthrough wherever you go and whatever you do!

Chapter Two

THE BREAKER HAS COME

The Breaker [the Messiah] will go up before them. They will break through, pass in through the gate and go out through it, and their King will pass on before them, the Lord at their head (Micah 2:13 AMP).

I could hear the sound of what seemed like thousands marching, as someone with a loud voice was shouting out commands, leading them. This vision or dream was so real that I actually thought I was right in the middle of what I saw happening. I turned to see what the noise was and who was speaking. Suddenly, the sound of the marching feet stopped, and I could see the leader off in the distance. It was a man, and he was walking toward me. Soon, standing within a few feet of me was a man with a beard and mustache dressed in a white T-shirt and combat fatigues. He was looking directly at me with such a look of intensity!

"What's the matter, don't you recognize me?" he asked. Surprised, I replied, "Jesus? I didn't know it was you!" I didn't recognize Him as He was dressed in an outfit that I would have never thought He would be wearing. It was not your normal picture of what you would imagine the Lord Jesus wearing! However, He then smiled, and said, "Hank, to Ezekiel I was the wheel within the wheel; to Moses, I was the burning bush; and to Joshua I was the captain of the hosts. Which one of them was right in their understanding of Me?" I answered, "Well, Lord, I guess they were all right." He then said, "That's right, because,

I will reveal and manifest myself the way that I choose and according to the generation that I am reaching."

Breakthrough Revelation

I was completely surprised and humbled! I didn't recognize the Lord who came to me as a commander of an army dressed like a modern-day drill instructor. I really shouldn't have been surprised that He was shown to me differently than I had expected, as He is the breaker that goes ahead of His people, leading them into breakthrough!

It completely was against my religious understanding and interpretation of who He was and what He was supposed to look like. However, I had to pause and realize that the Bible does say the Lord is a warrior (see Exod. 15:3), so I suppose it wouldn't be biblically wrong to see Him dressed in various types of military apparel!

This is why I believe many good-hearted and good-intended people don't get a breakthrough or never break through any barriers in their lives. It is because they have a preconceived mind-set, like I did, as to how Jesus should act or what He may look like. We often don't look at the biblical persona of Jesus. We often relate to Him according to movies, paintings, stories, sermons, how we were raised, or how we think that He should be based on our own personal experiences. All of them may be correct, but it is often one dimensional or limited from the full and true revelation or understanding of Jesus. He wants us to understand how vast He is and how He can meet every need of man by the different names and descriptions that He is called.

An example of this can be found in the book of Revelation. Jesus was not just described in human form seated at the right hand of God, but we see Him being also described as a lamb. Revelation 5:6 (NKJV) says:

And I looked, and behold, in the midst of the throne and of the four living creatures, and in the midst of the elders, stood a Lamb as though it had been slain, having seven horns and seven eyes, which are the seven Spirits of God sent out into all the earth.

However, notice He wasn't just described as a lamb, but specifically as the Lamb of God who was slain. This event was in the Throne Room. We know Jesus is in the form of a glorified Man, but in this example He appears differently as the slain Lamb of God.

After Jesus rose from the dead, the disciples had the same problem of receiving Him in a form different from their previous experience. They had a preconceived mind-set and were full of unbelief. This hindered them from breaking a mind-set barrier that Jesus had indeed risen from the dead. In many of the examples of His appearing after His crucifixion and resurrection, the disciples and Mary Magdalene didn't recognize Him when He appeared.

> *And when she had thus said, she turned herself back, and saw Jesus standing, and knew not that it was Jesus* (John 20:14).

> *But when the morning was now come, Jesus stood on the shore: but the disciples knew not that it was Jesus* (John 21:4).

This was due in part to their unbelief about the fact that He actually would rise from the dead. However, their inability to recognize Him was also because of their preconceived mind-set about what Jesus looked like. Surely, their last image of Him, especially seeing Him being disfigured beyond human recognition when He died, affected them.

> *Just as there were many who were appalled at Him His appearance was so disfigured beyond that of any man and His form marred beyond human likeness* (Isaiah 52:14 NIV).

Undoubtedly, the difference of how He appeared before and during the crucifixion was considerably different from how He looked after His glorious resurrection! They had never seen Him as the glorified, resurrected Lord of all.

Another example to further this point is when they locked the doors and hid in the upper room in fear just after the crucifixion.

Then the same day at evening, being the first day of the week, when the doors were shut where the disciples were assembled for fear of the Jews, came Jesus and stood in the midst, and saith unto them, Peace be unto you (John 20:19).

Now keep in mind that some of the disciples had already seen Jesus alive and they had reports that He was indeed resurrected. Yet, here they were hiding out, fearful of the Jews. It is apparent that the last image of the Jews mocking Him and demanding His death was still the predominant image branded on their minds. They obviously weren't expecting anything miraculous even though they already heard Jesus was alive! It seems clear that they weren't planning for Jesus to show up at all, and most certainly not appear out of nowhere! Still Thomas had so branded a certain image in His mind that He didn't initially believe it was Jesus. Even after Jesus supernaturally found their location *and* entered the room out of thin air, they couldn't take on a new mind-set.

Their view was one-dimensional, restrictive, and filled with doubt and fear. Jesus also appeared in a different way other than through the door, further stretching their way of thinking. We often do the same type of thing, and it hinders our breakthrough. We lock Jesus out and limit Him to our restrictive understanding and ways. We try to limit Him to our realm of understanding. Jesus just appearing, rather than walking through the door, is not what they were expecting. God often doesn't break through or reveal Himself in the natural way we expect or determine. If the disciples were to be barrier breakers who would advance His Church, they needed to increase their belief, revelation, and understanding of Him in order to break through for the Gospel. Jesus just appearing, rather than using the door, would help them to break a barrier in their mind and expectations.

God wants us to increase in our revelation of Him and not be limited in our understanding of either Him or His power. This is why I believe God described Himself using so many different names and descriptions throughout Scripture. When God introduced Himself to Moses, He told him His name was, "I am that I am!" (see Exod. 3:14). By this statement, God was saying, "Moses, I am everything that you, humankind, and all the earth will ever need."

God identifying Himself as the "I am" was giving all His attributes in one word, saying, "I am everything." He has given so many different names and revelations of Himself to better help us recognize who He is and what He can do! The greater our understanding of Him, and the more we declare Him as such, the more mental barriers are broken in the process!

Below are just a few examples from Scripture of how God chooses to identify Himself. These help us better understand His character and aid us in breaking through barriers in our lives.

- ADONAI: "Lord" (see Gen. 15:2). In the Old Testament, Yahweh is more often used in the Lord's dealings with His people, the Jews. Adonai is used more when He deals with the Gentiles.

- YAHWEH/JEHOVAH: "Lord" (see Deut. 6:4).

- YAHWEH-SABAOTH: "The Lord of Hosts" (see Isa. 1:24).

- JEHOVAH-JIREH: "The Lord will Provide" (see Gen. 22:14).

- JEHOVAH-M'KADDESH: "The Lord Who Sanctifies, Makes Holy" (see Lev. 20:8).

- JEHOVAH-NISSI: "The Lord Our Banner" (see Exod. 17:15).

- JEHOVAH-RAPHA: "The Lord Who Heals" (see Exod. 15:26).

- JEHOVAH ROHI: "The Lord Our Shepherd" (see Ps. 23:1).

- JEHOVAH-SHALOM: "The Lord Our Peace" (see Judg. 6:24).

- JEHOVAH-SHAMMAH: "The Lord is There" (see Ezek. 48:35).

- JEHOVAH-TSIDKENU: "Lord Our Righteousness" (see Jer. 33:16).

- EL ELYON: "Most High" (see Deut. 26:19).

- EL OHIM: God "Creator, Mighty and Strong" (see Jer. 31:33).

- ELOLAM: "Everlasting God" (see Ps. 90:1-3).

- EL ROI: "God of Seeing" (see Gen. 16:13).

- EL SHADDAI: "God Almighty" (see Gen. 49:24).

In each of these examples, we can declare Him according to His name and attributes. He is so mighty and amazing that not one word or characterization of Him is enough! We need to declare Him as these things because whatever we declare God as, He will come like a magnet and manifest Himself accordingly.

An example of this would be when you know Him and declare Him as JEHOVAH-JIREH, which means "the Lord will provide," in your times of need. When you declare Him as that, you will begin to receive revelation that God will break through and be faithful to provide for you. You decreeing Him as your provider draws this attribute of Him to your life for breakthrough! He shows Himself strong as your provision because you have declared Him to be such. Therefore, that is what He will become for you. This is why the Bible says decree a thing and it will be established. *"Thou shalt also decree a thing, and it shall be established unto thee: and the light shall shine upon thy ways"* (Job 22:28).

Obviously, this Scripture is speaking in reference to what we speak, but it also implies what we decree of God as well. Whichever name you choose to say and speak about God, according to your revelation, then that is what He is. When you call Him JEHOVAH-SHAMMAH, which means "the Lord is there," He becomes JEHOVAH-SHAMMAH to you and you will have the blessing of His presence. When you call Him JEHOVAH-RAPHA, "the Lord of our health," then the healing power of God begins to come forth. Whichever attribute you call God by, He manifests accordingly to what you declare.

The Breaker Has Come!

One of the ways that God is manifesting Himself today is as the Breaker! This is the fulfillment of the prophecy of Genesis 3:15 that we discussed in Chapter 1 concerning a Serpent Crusher coming! Yes, the Serpent Crusher is Jesus, the Breaker! He breaks down all the powers of the evil one. All through Scripture we see the powerful nature of God breaking through for His people, all of it foreshadowing that the Breaker was coming in Jesus Christ. All through history we see in the Scriptures before Jesus the Breaker came to earth that the prophets foretold of His coming and kept declaring through the centuries, "He's coming! He's coming!"

This is why when we understand Him and declare Him as the Breaker or the Lord of the breakthrough, it attracts Him to our situation like a magnet!

You see, Jesus is the master of breakthrough. He has come! He is what the prophets foretold!

> *The breaker is come up before them: they have broken up, and have passed through the gate, and are gone out by it: and their king shall pass before them and the LORD on the head of them* (Micah 2:13).

We understand from this verse, and also from Genesis 3:15, the prophecy that the Breaker has come. The NIV version gives us an additional understanding of this Breaker. Micah 2:13 says:

> *One who breaks open the way will go up before them; they will break through the gate and go out. Their king will pass through before them, the LORD at their head.*

This verse in the NIV states that the Lord will break open the way for us. It also says that He will help us to break through by preparing the way for us to break through! We need the Breaker, the Lord of the breakthrough, because we can't have breakthrough without Him.

We must get this revelation of the Lord, who is the Breaker, in order to position ourselves for a breakthrough. My intent is to progressively brand this image of Him upon your mind throughout this book. Once we receive the revelation of who He is and what He has revealed of Himself by His attributes and the names He has used to identify himself, it better positions us to break barriers in our lives.

Let's look at this verse again and examine just what it means, for you and me, that the Breaker, God, has come.

> *I will surely assemble, O Jacob, all of thee; I will surely gather the remnant of Israel; I will put them together as the sheep of Bozrah, As the flock in the midst of their fold: they shall make great noise by reason of the multitude of men. The breaker is come up before them: they have broken up, and have passed through the gate, and are gone out by it: and their king shall pass before them, and the LORD on the head of them* (Micah 2:12-13).

In these verses, the Scripture references the sheep of Bozrah and their sheepfold and how the Breaker goes on ahead of them. The sheepfold that was seen in biblical times was often made out of stone. Inside these sheepfolds the sheep would be protected and confined by their shepherd for their own protection. This was especially true at night. There were even times when the shepherd would lay in front of the sheepfold's only door so he would know if either the sheep tried to leave or a predator tried to enter. At the break of day, the shepherd would come into the sheepfold among his sheep. When it was dawn, the sheep would often gather around the shepherd as he prepared to open a way for them to leave the sheepfold. He then opened the door, making a way for them as he was delivering them from the stone enclosure. As soon as the shepherd would open the way for the sheep to go out, they would gather together alongside the shepherd pushing up against the way out with a lot of force. This is the same analogy we find in the Book of Matthew concerning those in the Kingdom of God. *"The kingdom of heaven suffers* [allows] *violence and the violent* [are pressing in to] *take it by force"* (Matt. 11:12 NKJV).

We who are born again into the Kingdom of God must have this same kind of breakthrough spirit we saw in the sheep at Bozrah. This is especially true since Jesus made the way for us, and now we need to press in and claim what is rightfully ours just like the sheep at Bozrah!

When the breakthrough came for the whole flock in the sheepfold, these sheep would pour out of the sheepfold through the opening together with the shepherd who was leading them as he went before them. They would follow their shepherd as he led them out to find pasture. This is a great picture of how Jesus the Breaker brings us out to prepare the way for us leading us from a place of confinement into green pastures of blessing! Another scriptural example to help us better understand the Breaker, Jesus, and the sheep of Bozrah can be found in the book of Isaiah. Isaiah 42:6-7 (NIV) says:

> *I, the LORD, have called you in righteousness; I will take hold of your hand. I will keep you and will make you to be a covenant for the people and a light for the Gentiles, to open eyes that are blind, to free captives from prison and to release from the dungeon those who sit in darkness.*

This verse again reveals that Jesus will lead us by the hand and free us like the sheep of Bozrah. He takes us from a place of bondage and breaks through for us, leading us to victory. God is telling us something about these sheep at Bozrah that also relates to those who are barrier breakers. The Scripture in Micah that is referring to the sheep of Bozrah is very important because it is a picture of deliverance and the return of Jesus Christ. It also speaks of breakthrough, victory, and deliverance for those who are sheep in the Kingdom of God. The picture we need to see of this wonderful Lord Jesus, the Breaker, is one who will be coming to break out His people! This Bozrah deliverance is a great example of the deliverance that the Breaker brings for His people. Jesus, and Jesus alone, is "the Breaker." This is why the Holy Spirit inspired the prophet Micah to declare God as the Breaker.

To help us better understand the picture of what is being portrayed for us concerning breakthrough is to study the definition of the word *breaker* in the Hebrew. The Hebrew definition for the word *breaker* is "parats" (paw-rats). This definition means "to breakthrough, abroad, make a breach, break away, burst out, come spread abroad, compel, disperse and to grow."[1]

Other definitions for the word *breaker* and *parats* are "down or over, to break or burst out from womb or enclosure, to break into, to break open and break in pieces, to break out (violently)."

All of these definitions give us better insight to how God the Breaker will work on our behalf!

We see this also when Jesus began His ministry and walked in the temple and read out of the book of Isaiah. It looked like a harmless reading of Scripture, but it was more than that! He was declaring that He was the Breaker, the Anointed One who came to break through every barrier we would face! Of course, the religious demons in the scribes and Pharisees couldn't handle that the Messiah, the Breaker, had come. They didn't like that He was declaring the breakthrough that would come for the people. The Pharisees and the demons in them were so angry at this announcement they actually sought to kill Jesus. Luke 4:28-30 says:

And all they in the synagogue, when they heard these things, were filled with wrath, and rose up, and thrust Him out of the city, and led Him unto the brow of the hill whereon their city was built, that they might cast Him down headlong. But He passing through the midst of them went His way. . . .

They sought to stop the Breaker from manifesting and to stop the breakthroughs that He was declaring from coming. Jesus was declaring He was anointed for breakthrough concerning you and all humankind! Notice what the Breaker, Jesus, declared. He declared He would break through for you! Luke 4:18–19 says:

The Spirit of the Lord is upon Me, because He hath anointed Me to preach the gospel to the poor; He hath sent Me to heal the brokenhearted, to preach deliverance to the captives, and recovering of sight to the blind, to set at liberty them that are bruised, to preach the acceptable year of the Lord.

Notice in each of these decrees from the Breaker it deals with what we face in life spiritually, physically, and emotionally. That pretty much covers it all! The preaching of the gospel always deals with and brings deliverance and healing to humankind emotionally, spiritually, and physically.

- Emotionally—heal the brokenhearted and set at liberty those that are bruised.
- Spiritually—deliverance to the captives.
- Physically—recovery of sight to the blind.

It shouldn't surprise us that God is the Breaker and will break through in every area of our lives. His very nature is that of breakthrough! He manifested Himself as a Breaker, a warrior taking on Pharaoh and his entire army single handily. So much was the routing of Pharaoh and his armies that the children of Israel began to sing, declare, and praise the Lord who is a warrior!

Exodus 15:1,3-4 says:

Then sang Moses and the children of Israel this song unto the LORD, and spake, saying, I will sing unto the LORD, for He hath triumphed gloriously: the horse and his rider hath He thrown into the sea. . . . The LORD is a man of war: the LORD is His name. Pharaoh's chariots and his host hath He cast into the sea: his chosen captains also are drowned in the Red Sea.

They were declaring these things because He *is* a warrior. It is His nature, and He is a man of war. When the Lord returns, He is pictured as a mighty warrior, a Breaker who establishes His Kingdom forever and is coming to rule over the nations. He is coming to make war and to break through for His people (see Rev. 19). This should be an encouragement to you as you understand just who you have in your corner fighting for you. You have the Breaker, the warrior, the Lord Jesus Himself!

Let me tell you about a powerful vision I once had. It was during a worship service at Lord of Hosts Church, which I pastor in Omaha, Nebraska. I was standing and worshiping the Lord when all of a sudden everything in front of my eyes changed. I heard a noise that sounded like galloping horse's hooves. I looked up and soon became part of a spiritual vision. I saw a big, beautiful, powerful, and muscular horse just a few feet in front of me. I noticed the feet and legs of the person riding it, so I continued to raise my eyes up, looking to see who was riding this magnificent horse. I immediately realized that it was Jesus, and He was dressed in what looked like a huge Indian headdress. He looked at me, and the next thing I knew, He threw a huge, feathered spear right down at my feet.

I must admit this vision, like the one I wrote about earlier when Jesus came dressed in combat fatigues, messed with my religious mind. I thought, *Why would Jesus come dressed riding on a horse with a huge Indian chief headdress?* Shortly after this vision, I read in the Bible that Jesus is called the Chief Shepherd. First Peter 5:4 says, *"And when the chief Shepherd shall appear, ye shall receive a crown of glory that fadeth not away."*

He is the Chief. He is King of all, Lord of all, and Chief of all. I am not sure why He chose the headdress of an Indian type of chief, but I do know that He is the Chief Warrior and Breaker!

God broke through the darkness when He said let there be light, and when nothing was visible He made it visible. He made something out of nothing! If God did this when He created everything that was created, how much more will He break through for you? The earth was dark and void, yet God broke through! This same condition of the dark and void earth may be similar to what you are facing. Remember, if God could break through at that time, He will break through now for you!

The Breaker Must Go Before Us!

If we want the Lord to break through our darkness and feeling of emptiness, or just to have overall breakthrough, then we must develop the same breakthrough spirit of the sheep of Bozrah that we read about a few pages earlier. Again, this comes by receiving and understanding who the Lord is and by declaring Him as such. We then need to allow the Breaker, the Lord Himself, to go before us if we are going to experience a breakthrough. Let's examine again Micah 2:13: *"The breaker is come up before them...."*

Notice that the Breaker must go before us! Do you know why He must go before us? What does it really mean for the Lord to go before us? It means that He is the one who will go before us in victory by breaking through any obstacle or barrier in our lives. He is the God of the breakthrough.

He goes ahead of us and prepares the way, leading us into victory. In every situation, He will come through because He is our Breaker, the one who brings the breakthrough on our behalf. It is vital that we allow Him to go before us and not try to go ahead of Him. If we will allow Him to break through for us, He will clear the way and lead us into the victory we desire. He is like a blocker in a football game plowing through the defensive line. Defensive blockers open holes and flatten opponents as they prepare the way for the one carrying the ball to gain yards and score a touchdown. God is like this blocker as He goes before you so you can win in the game of life!

The Breaker will begin to intervene in every circumstance of our lives, but we must let Him go before us. It is important that we don't get ahead of Him but rather let Him go ahead of us to break open the way for us to come through.

King David had to learn the importance of knowing God as the Breaker and letting Him lead the way. This was true if he was to have victory over the Philistines.

We see this in Second Samuel 5. When the Philistines heard that David became the king, they decided to try to fight him in the valley of Rephaim.

David, hearing of the enemy, began to ask the Lord whether he should attack them or not. The Lord answered David affirmatively that he was to attack. This inquiring of the Lord brought a victory for David. He also received a revelation of the Lord as the Lord of the breakthrough. He declared that the Lord broke through upon his enemies and called the place Baal-perazim, which means "the place of breakthrough." *"The LORD hath broken forth upon mine enemies before me, as the breach of waters. Therefore he called the name of that place Baalperazim"* (2 Sam. 5:20).

After this victory, the Philistines attacked again, and the Lord told David to do something that is vital for us when we are praying and believing for breakthrough. God told David to wait until he heard the sound of the wind blowing through the mulberry trees. When David heard this sound, it was a sign that the Breaker had gone before him, leading him to victory (see verses 23-25). David's wise choice of letting the Breaker go before him led to another great breakthrough victory!

This is exactly what happened when the wind of Pentecost in Acts 2 had finally come. The wind was the indication that Jesus had gone ahead of them and was seated at the right hand of God. It would later signify that not only had Jesus gone ahead and prepared the way for them, but now they could break through with the power of the Holy Ghost that had been poured out. It was a sign that breakthrough was coming and had actually come. As the 120 prayed in the Upper Room, the wind and shaking came as a result of breakthrough in the heavens. Their prayers released the Lord to go before them and for the Holy Spirit to bring the breakthrough.

We know this from the Greek word for wait, *perimeno*, used in Acts 1:4.

*And, being assembled together with them, commanded them that they should not depart from Jerusalem, but **wait** for the promise of the Father, which, saith He, ye have heard of Me.*

The word *peri* means "to pierce through the darkness" and the word *meno* means "to wait in a place of expectancy." They had prayed and allowed the wind of the Holy Spirit to break through!

From David's account, we can see just how important it is to let the Breaker go before us. One of the ways we can let the Breaker go before us is by our worship and praise. When we praise the Lord, He moves against our enemies. We see this in Judges 1, as the Lord told Joshua to send the tribe of Judah first into battle. Judah means "praise" in the Hebrew. So you could say, "When you send praise first, the battle will be won!" Judah went first, and it released the Breaker to go on ahead and gave victory again to the people. This was also true of Jehoshaphat and the people who were surrounded by the enemy. All Jehoshaphat had to do was send his singers praising and worshiping ahead of him. This would create a sound that would bring the Breaker on the scene. It was when they chose to praise God that He sent an ambush against the enemy (see 2 Chron. 20:22-23).

Moses and Israel also allowed the Breaker to go before them as a pillar of cloud by day, and as a result, the armies of Egypt were completely wiped out at the crossing of the Red Sea. They never saw these enemies again! Then there were Joshua and Israel marching around the walls of Jericho. The Lord told Joshua that He would go before him as the Captain of the Host and give them victory if they would let Him go before them. They were told to march around the walls once each day for six days and then on the seventh day to march around seven times and then shout. That is a total of 13 times! It is often suggested that the number 13 is always unlucky or bad; however, in this case it represented the number for breakthrough! They got a breakthrough because they let the Breaker go before them!

Again, the key in breaking barriers and receiving a breakthrough is allowing God to go before us, and we see the result of it in Isaiah 45:2-3:

I will go before thee, and make the crooked places straight: I will break in pieces the gates of brass, and cut in sunder the bars of iron: and I will give thee the treasures of darkness, and hidden riches of secret places, that thou mayest know that I, the LORD, which call thee by thy name, am the God of Israel.

God breaks things open before you and straightens things out! When we pursue God in prayer, His Word, and praise and worship, it releases the sound that the Breaker hears that moves on your behalf. He comes as the Breaker to bring you the victory you need no matter what is against you or how powerful the attacks may be against you! The key is let Him go before you when you do your part to praise and seek Him! Look to the Breaker and not always to what man can do!

Progressing in Breakthrough Revelation

It is so important to get a true understanding of who God is and how He chooses to manifest Himself. This is especially true when it comes to understanding the Lord as the Breaker. It is imperative to let the Breaker go ahead of you, leading you into breakthrough. To do this it requires you to continue to progress in your pursuit and understanding of the Lord. This is why David was able to defeat Goliath, because he let the Breaker go ahead and progressed in his revelation of God as the victory. We know this because David progressed in the revelation of God before he killed Goliath, and it was this revelation that helped him break through. Remember David's words before defeating Goliath. He mentioned the previous times that God broke through for him by killing a lion and a bear! First Samuel 17:37 says:

David said moreover, The LORD that delivered me out of the paw of the lion, and out of the paw of the bear, He will deliver me out of the hand of this Philistine. . . .

We see from Scripture how important it is that we understand and have a revelation of God that is not just one-dimensional or limited. We need our revelation of God to expand and progress.

When positioning yourself for breakthrough, it is key to get a revelation of God that isn't just based on what others have said. Revelation of God progresses and grows by spending personal time with Him that lines up with Scripture. It comes to you by the Word of God and the Spirit of God. Another way to receive revelation is to find a good, Bible-believing church and pastor who preaches God's Word and allows the Lord to manifest as He did many times and ways in Scripture. It is interesting to note that when Jesus was born in the earth that God chose shepherds. Why shepherds? I believe it is because they are a prophetic shadow of how a good, godly pastor can lead us to a true godly revelation of Jesus that is both fresh and progressive. God uses pastors/ shepherds to grow us in the knowledge and understanding of the Lord. There is also safety in this because when people think they have some special, all-inclusive revelation, they get in danger of being deceived. They need a good church and pastor to counter them and balance their beliefs.

Jesus came to the earth differently from what the Israelites expected. They didn't recognize their Messiah, their deliverer, because they had a preconceived mind-set as to how He should come. They couldn't allow God to expand their understanding. It is interesting to note that when Jesus first came to the earth, He was born in a feeding trough. Again, very different than what was expected. It didn't look significant at all, but it was because it was the King of kings born to die for all. When it comes to receiving breakthrough, it may not be how we expect it, or appear significant in any way, so we don't recognize it as the process of breakthrough. This is why the apostle Paul said, he was praying for the Church at Ephesus to receive more revelation of God. Ephesians 1:17 says:

> *That the God of our Lord Jesus Christ, the Father of glory, may give unto you the spirit of wisdom and revelation in the knowledge of Him. . . .*

There is a need to receive revelation of God for yourself if you are going to be a successful barrier breaker. In Matthew 16, we see that this was true when Jesus met His disciples with a question regarding His identity.

Matthew 16:13 (NIV) says, *"Jesus came to the region of Caesarea Philippi, He asked His disciples, 'Who do people say the Son of Man is?'"* The question Jesus was asking was related to what men say of Him. In verse 14 we see the different responses of the disciples: *"They replied, 'Some say John the Baptist; others say Elijah; and still others, Jeremiah or one of the prophets'"* (NIV).

Their good-intended answers revealed that in their heart and understanding they didn't have a real revelation of Jesus for themselves, but rather, it was based on what others were saying. Jesus was trying to get them to progress in their revelation of who He was and what He came to do. Their responses didn't satisfy Jesus and what He was looking for. So, Jesus asked a more direct question that didn't have to do with what others were saying but with the revelation they personally had of Him. *"'But what about you?" He asked. "Who do you say I am?'"* (Matt. 16:15 NIV).

Again, the disciples could all quote what others said about Jesus but didn't have a revelation for themselves. This sounds like a lot of people today! There was only one disciple who had a revelation of who Jesus was for them. It was Peter; he was the only one who received the revelation by himself from God the Father.

> *Simon Peter answered, "You are the Christ, the Son of the living God." Jesus replied, "Blessed are you, Simon son of Jonah, for this was not revealed to you by man, but by My Father in heaven.* (Matthew 16:16-17 NIV).

Peter had to receive a revelation of Jesus that was not just based on what others had revealed, but one that carried personal understanding. His revelation, Jesus said, came only because the Father revealed it. It didn't come by human flesh and blood alone. This revelation was so powerful that Jesus said of that revelation, or rock, that the gates of hell would not prevail against it.

> *"And I tell you that you are Peter, and on this rock I will build My church, and the gates of Hades will not overcome it. I will give you the keys of the kingdom*

of heaven; whatever you bind on earth will be bound in heaven, and whatever you loose on earth will be loosed in heaven" (Matthew 16:18-19 NIV).

Jesus was saying that the devil and his demons can't prevail against the revelation of God and who He truly is that you have gained for yourself. This is so important for breakthrough. When you have this revelation, you will bind and loose things in the heavens and upon earth. Binding and loosing are necessary actions of revelation to bring breakthrough and to break barriers in your life. This revelation brings a confidence to approach God's throne boldly and confidently with an authority to break through every demonic barrier that is against you. As you progress in your revelation of God and develop a greater understanding of Him, then you can break through the devil's barriers.

Peter's revelation of Jesus was not a one-time event or just for that moment. He still had to progress in his revelation of Jesus Christ so he could break through with the keys of the Kingdom that he had been given. He continued in his revelation of Jesus, especially as the healer, and the more revelation he received, the greater the breakthrough results!

- *Peter at the gate Beautiful.* A crippled beggar waited daily at the gate expecting to receive alms of Peter and John. Acts 3:6 says,

  "Then Peter said, 'Silver and gold have I none; but such as I have give I thee: In the name of Jesus Christ of Nazareth rise up and walk.'"

  Peter uses the name of Jesus as he ministers to the man. He told him to rise and walk in the name of Jesus.

- *Peter praying for a man named Aeneas.* Acts 9:33-34 says,

  "And there he found a certain man named Aeneas, which had kept his bed eight years, and was sick of the palsy. And Peter said unto him, Aeneas, Jesus Christ maketh thee whole: arise, and make thy bed. And he arose immediately."

  The next thing Peter did as he progressed in breakthrough revelation and healing was instead of using the name of Jesus, as he did in the previous example (and as we can do also to receive our healing), he just declared that Jesus Christ had made this man whole.

- *Peter raises a woman named Tabitha from the dead.* Acts 9:40-41 says,

  "But Peter put them all forth, and kneeled down, and prayed; and turning him to the body said, Tabitha, arise. And she opened her eyes: and when she saw Peter, she sat up. And he gave her his hand, and lifted her up, and when he had called the saints and widows, presented her alive."

  And finally the revelation had progressed so much that Peter just spoke with the same power and authority of His Lord, Jesus. He didn't say "in the name of Jesus" or pray. Again, if he did and had faith in the name and in his prayer, he would get results; but he had such a revelation of who he was in Christ and the power made available to him that he just spoke, "Arise!" This is the same way it works for you and me.

All who want to be true barrier breakers with supernatural results need to keep progressing in their faith. It will require diligence in seeking God and staying close to His Word. When we spend time with God, we are changed and will continue to progress in our understanding of Him, as vast as He is. Second Corinthians 3:18 says:

> But we all, with open face beholding as in a glass the glory of the Lord, are changed into the same image from glory to glory, even as by the Spirit of the Lord.

Notice it is a progressive revelation of God, from glory to glory. This is why the angels surrounding God's throne in Heaven never stop saying, "Holy, Holy, Holy, is the Lord." I believe they continue to do this because each time they see God they get a new and greater revelation of Him in His holiness. If we want to continue to progress in our revelation of God, it will require a willingness to step out of our comfort zone in obedience to the Lord.

I personally was determined to progress in revelation and understanding of who God is as Jehovah Rapha, the Lord our health. I began to make small steps to start praying for people who were sick, and especially those who were crippled. I meditated on Jesus, our healer, and read the many examples of healing

Scriptures that are made available to us today. I was armed with a faith and revelation of God from several weeks of getting the Word in my heart and was ready to take bolder steps in my effort to pray for the sick. My wife, Brenda, and I went on a cruise and decided to go shopping as the ship was docked. We entered into a store and the usual happened: my wife got excited as she saw all the great items for sale, while I immediately became glazed over and looked for the nearest place to sit down while she shopped. I couldn't find a place to sit, so I just stood by the front of the store. I immediately noticed my chance to progress in my revelation of healing, as right in front me was a young man, probably in his late 20s or early 30s, sitting in a wheelchair.

In my mind, I began to strategize how I could lead a conversation into an opportunity to pray for him and get him out of that wheelchair. I started with some small talk, asking where he was from, and to my surprise, he lived only a few miles away from Omaha, where I lived. I rejoiced in my heart that God had set this up with a man who only lived a few miles away, and I was convinced that God was setting up a miracle. I was going to let the Breaker go before me and do a miracle. The conversation was progressing well for quite some time, and I could tell the man was enjoying it. I started to progress even more. I told this man that I was a pastor and we had been having powerful healing miracles in our church. I then began to tell him how God still heals today and that God would do a miracle in his life too. I was ready to make my move and ask him if I could lay my hand on him and pray to lift him out of that chair. I was ready for a lame man to walk when suddenly, as I was ready to pray, I heard a woman say, "Are you ready?" I turned to see who it was; it appeared to be his wife, so I thought, *I better move fast and pray for him.* However, as quickly as I had thought it, the man in the wheelchair replied, "Yes!" and got out of the wheelchair and walked out of the store. I stood stunned and embarrassed as I quickly realized my healing revival had been ended by a man who was not crippled at all. He was merely sitting in the wheelchair that just happened to be there while his wife shopped! I had fallen right into it, and the man was having fun with it at my expense. I must admit that after it happened, I felt like a fool, but I quickly realized how far I had progressed. I was actually ready to be bold and pray for someone to get out of a wheelchair in public! It helps me today to be bold and led by the Spirit more in what I do, especially in miracles. If I hadn't been willing to step out and progress, I may not have the success I am seeing today by the Spirit of God.

Many times the greatest barriers we have to break are in our own minds. When we truly understand who God is and how He chooses to manifest Himself in every generation, then we will see the breakthroughs we desire. This is why there are so many different denominations. It is important to have the present truth of what the Holy Spirit is speaking. Second Peter 1:12 says:

> *Wherefore I will not be negligent to put you always in remembrance of these things, though ye know them, and be established in the present truth.*

The reason many don't progress is because each camp or denomination often thinks their revelation is the most correct or most relevant for today. Some are unwilling to change or come into a greater revelation of God and His Word. This keeps the Breaker from progressing and bringing greater breakthroughs. Many times the revelation or the relevancy is based on something that came generations ago. This often keeps people from progressing and never advancing in their understanding of God. I am not saying that we walk away or change the basic doctrines of our Christian faith, but rather that we don't become limited in our revelation of God and His Word. The scribes and Pharisees never came to the revelation or understanding that Jesus was the true Messiah. Yet they should have because they had more of the Word of God than any others, as it was part of their religious education.

There are also those who refuse to move forward with how God reveals Himself because they want to hold on to the old. Jesus called it old wine and old wine skins. He was referring to the Scribes and Pharisees. He was saying that God was doing something new and relevant in the earth and they failed to progress with Him. This happened also with Israel when God had to tell them to quit going around the mountain. They were going around Mount Seer, just wandering and maintaining in a 40-year-old revelation, and they weren't progressing. God was trying to get them to keep pursuing, but in order to do that He had to have a whole generation die off so Israel could receive their promise.

"And the LORD spake unto me, saying, Ye have compassed this mountain long enough: turn you northward"(Deut. 2:2-3).

Even when God reveals Himself in a way other than what we expect, His revelation lines up with Scripture. We must be careful that we don't think our revelation is all inclusive or the only right one. We have to progress from glory to glory and faith to faith. This is what God was saying to Joshua when He told him that Moses was dead, but every place that Joshua's feet would tread God would give him that land (see Josh. 1:1-5). God never revealed himself to Moses as the Captain of the Hosts, but He did to Joshua. God was telling Joshua, "You need to take what I revealed and how I revealed Myself in the prior generation with Moses and realize he is dead, and I may not be emphasizing certain things as I did with Moses with you. However, Joshua, you still meditate day and night on the word that I gave to you and Israel under Moses and progress in the promise that every place you go I will give the ground to you."

How do you receive a greater revelation and understanding of God to help break through in your life? It always starts by a pursuit of intimacy with God through prayer. It is also imperative to stay deeply committed and rooted in the Bible to help you understand the nature and character of God, as seen in the different Scripture examples. We need to keep seeking, studying, and declaring who God is. Our spiritual hunger and pursuit of His heart is so vital in understanding Him. God's heart, and not just a simple revelation alone, is enough. Peter had a revelation of God that came from the Heavenly Father, while the other disciples' revelation was based on what they heard and not a personal understanding.

John, one of Jesus' disciples, didn't just have a revelation but had something that was deeper and even more progressive. He had an intimate friendship with Jesus that indicated him being found leaning his head upon the breast of Jesus right next to His heartbeat. John 21:20 says, *"Then Peter, turning about, seeth the disciple whom Jesus loved following; which also leaned on His breast at supper...."*

This is significant in becoming a barrier breaker because the deeper your relationship and revelation is, the greater your breakthrough will be! Progressing in revelation of God is the foundation and necessity to better understand

Him. We must keep running after, pursuing, pressing in, and searching for God in our hearts. A good example of this is Peter and John running to an empty tomb when they heard that Jesus was alive. It reveals a lot about the importance of progressing with a spiritual hunger and pursuit of God for breakthrough. The Bible says that John outran Peter. John 20:3-4 says:

> *Peter therefore went forth, and that other disciple, and came to the sepulchre. So they ran both together: and the other disciple did outrun Peter, and came first to the sepulchre.*

Physically speaking, maybe John was faster than Peter. Yet there is a spiritual principle that must not be overlooked. John had the heart of Jesus, which can be seen in his leaning on Jesus' breast, while Peter had a revelation he had received of the Heavenly Father. Spiritually speaking, the one with God's heart will always break barriers or outrun those who only have, or are just seeking, a revelation of Him alone.

Progress Until Breakthrough Comes

The more you progress in your heart, the more you will know the God of the breakthrough and better position yourself to succeed in breaking through.

We can see throughout this chapter and the Scriptures that breakthrough can be progressive. It is often assumed that a breakthrough by its very nature happens immediately and all at once. An example of this is when David defeated some of the Philistines. Second Samuel 5:20 (AMP) says, *"The Lord has broken through my enemies before me, like the bursting out of great waters."* From this, our automatic assumption can be that victory breakthroughs are all immediate.

Webster's Dictionary defines a breakthrough as:

> **An offensive thrust that penetrates and carries beyond a defensive line in warfare or an act or instance of breaking through an obstacle; A sudden advance especially in knowledge or technique.**[2]

It is also defined as any significant or sudden advance or an act or instance of removing or surpassing an obstruction or restriction.

These definitions imply that breakthrough can be a sudden, significant thing. However, there is a progression and a process for it. Breakthrough is often like a game of American football. We celebrate the touchdown and put all of our focus on it, rather than what it took to score one. Yes, the touchdown was sudden, but what about all the plays and players that led to the touchdown? It is a progressive process. Breakthroughs are also too often considered to be immediate because we are so relieved when they come that our focus is solely on the breakthrough, and we don't consider or remember the process it took to get there. This is why so many quit or give up before receiving victory, because they are expecting immediate touchdowns or results.

The word *progressive* has a similar meaning to words like increasing, growing, intensifying, accelerating, escalating, developing, and cumulative. All of these speak of the process of breakthrough, as it often increases, grows, intensifies, and develops until it all accumulates and bursts forth. An old story I heard when I was young is a good example of this and will help you to better understand breakthrough and how the Lord broke through like the breaking forth of great waters.

You may have heard a similar story. It begins with a boy who saw a small hole in a dam. He noticed there was a small trickling of water leaking through the hole. The young boy in the story then stuck his finger in the hole to try and cut off the flow of water. He realized the whole city and dam would be safe as long as he held his finger in place. However, if he were to let go, because of the building water pressure, the dam would be at risk to burst and the whole city would be lost and the dam destroyed! The boy saved the whole city as well as saved the dam.

The moral of the story is if the boy hadn't stopped the trickle of water, it would soon have become a forceful stream, then from a steam to a raging current and from a raging current to a flood that would destroy everything in its path!

The breaking through of waters often starts with a trickle. This is what happened with David and the defeat of the Philistines. It progressed little by little the more David obeyed the Lord, until it became a mighty breakthrough like a flood of water breaking through a dam. But it didn't start that way; it started with a seed or a trickle! Again, breakthrough eventually increases, intensifies, and accumulates, as it often starts small and then progresses. It accelerates until it breaks through like water through a dam! This is important to understand so you don't throw in the towel and quit in the middle of the process, especially when it looks like nothing is happening. You might be in the early stages of your breakthrough, so stay encouraged and don't give up!

David's victory started off small and grew into a mighty breakthrough because he didn't quit and received a greater revelation of the Lord. He understood the Lord to be the "Lord of the breakthrough!" Second Samuel 5:20 (AMP) says:

> *The Lord has broken through my enemies before me, like the bursting out of great waters. So he called the name of that place Baal-perazim [Lord of breaking through].*

All through the Bible, we see that God broke through for His people, especially those who sought the Lord. To some the breakthroughs were immediate, while to others it was a process. In all of those who broke through to victory, they had to continue to endure and trust the word of the Breaker, which is God. This is important to understand, especially when it feels as though the breakthrough will never come. Remember all the times in Scripture that God broke through for His people and also all the times He has in your own life. Sometimes breakthrough doesn't manifest immediately and is dependent upon us not quitting in the process of what God has promised us. When it looks as if it will never come to pass, that's when you need to press on all the more, for God doesn't lie, nor will He. He will do what He has promised both in His Word and spoken to you by His Spirit. He needs you to believe Him and allow Him to break through in your situations. Look at those who could have given up when it looked like they would never break through any barriers, yet they did and so can you! They had to maintain their faith and trust in the living God and what He said!

- *Noah.* He progressed and broke through with a revelation of God and what the Lord told him even though it had never been done before. Noah, after being persecuted in his generation (see Luke 17), kept progressing year after year until breakthrough came in the form of rain.

- *Abraham and Sarah.* It was after 24 years that the promise of breakthrough came concerning them having a son (Isaac) together.

- *Joseph in Pharaoh's prison.* It was many years after Joseph's initial dream that he finally broke through, even when it looked like his dream was lost! He could have given up and forgotten as others did, yet he held on to his dream and received his breakthrough.

- *God sent plagues upon Egypt.* When it looked like His people would never get free of their bondage or captivity, He sent plagues to deliver them after 400 years!

- *Moses and Israel.* They crossed the Red Sea to receive their promised land. Their murmuring and complaining hindered their breakthrough and caused their promise to be delayed.

- *Joshua and the army of Israel standing before the walls of Jericho.* When it seemed like there were walls and giant barriers, they had to obey God for 7 days, marching around the barriers (or walls) of Jericho for a total of 13 times before the barriers (or breakthrough) took place.

- *David and Goliath.* Israel was threatened and mocked for 40 days by Goliath, and it seemed that all odds were against them. God brought a breakthrough with David that caused them to triumph with great victory!

- *Jehoshaphat.* He and the people were surrounded by the multitudes of Moabites and Ammonites and looked like they were in a hopeless situation. Yet God came and broke through, causing an ambush (see 1 Chron.).

- *Daniel in the lion's den.* God went before Daniel, and the Lord broke through on his behalf, stopping the mouths of the lions set to devour him in the lion's den.

- *Man at the pool of Bethesda.* He got his breakthrough after 38 years in his sickness; he received his breakthrough in a moment with one encounter with the Lord of the breakthrough, Jesus! He believed Jesus' words, and in an instant received his breakthrough of healing.

- *Woman with a spirit of infirmity.* This woman was bent over for 18 years before she received her promise of breakthrough. This doesn't imply that God heals some and others may have to wait or not get it all. Rather this woman was bound until the Breaker came and set her free. The awesome thing is Jesus has already gone before us on the cross and paid the price for our sin and diseases that we can receive breakthrough healing now (see 1 Pet. 1:2-4)! We are healed now!

I am certainly not suggesting that in order to break barriers or to break through into victory it always has to take an eternity, or at least seem like it. Rather, I am reminding you of the need to continue to press forward until breakthrough comes. From the examples given, we can see the importance of determination and endurance to bring the master of the breakthrough in our lives. You must let the Breaker go before you as you stay true and faithful to Him and what He has said to you.

When you understand that God is the Breaker and that He is the Lord of the breakthrough, you must let Him go before you to prepare the way like the shepherd at Bozrah. This progression always leads to a productive life of breakthroughs!

Endnotes

1. Blue Letter Bible. "Dictionary and Word Search for breaker (Strong's 6555)". Blue Letter Bible. 1996-2010. 10 Aug 2010. <http://www.blueletterbible.org/lang/lexicon/lexicon. cfm? Strongs=H6555&t=KJV >

2. "breakthrough." Merriam-Webster Online Dictionary. 2010. http:// www.merriam-webster.com (11 August 2010).

Chapter Three

DETERMINED FOR BREAKTHROUGH

Bitterly she weeps at night, tears are upon her cheeks. Among all her lovers there is none to comfort her. All her friends have betrayed her; they have become her enemies (Lamentations 1:2).

She weeps through the night with tears flowing down her cheeks. She has also been betrayed by her friends. This sounds a lot like someone in need of a breakthrough. This verse in Lamentations describes exactly how a woman in the Bible, Tamar, felt when she desired to have a child because her previous husband had died. It was the dream of many women, who were part of the covenant with Israel, to have their womb bring forth the promised Messiah, the Breaker that was prophesied in Genesis 3:15. This prophecy declared that the Messiah would arise through the womb of a woman and break forth to crush the head of the serpent, the devil. He was to be the ultimate deliverer of Israel. The Lord put the prophecy's fulfillment into motion by choosing a righteous man, Abraham, to begin the lineage that would produce the Messiah. God promised him that through his seed or family line all the nations of the earth would be blessed because from his bloodline the Breaker would arise. The process to bring this Breaker and serpent crusher forth would have to come through Abraham, his son Isaac, grandson Jacob, and his sons thereafter. God chose one of the twelve sons of Jacob, who was named Judah, and his descendents to be the family that this promised Breaker, Jesus Christ, would come from.

Knowing this was God's promise, you can imagine how many Israelite women desired to be the one chosen to carry this royal seed.

Tamar was one such a woman. Her story is found in Genesis 38. She was a widow who wanted a child and would do anything to have one. You could certainly say she needed a personal breakthrough. We will find that even though she used wrong methods according to moral standards to bring forth a child, God honored her because she believed in what belonged to her and was determined to obtain it. Her determination to take what was rightfully her own carries spiritual truths that we need to glean for birthing our own breakthrough.

In Need of a Breakthrough

To begin the story of Tamar, she was a young Jewish woman who married into a family through an arrangement made by her father-in-law, Judah. She was hoping desperately for children after marrying Judah's firstborn son, Er. Yet, in great disappointment, she didn't conceive a child. The Bible says Er was a wicked man in the sight of the Lord, so the Lord slew him.

With the death of her husband leaving her childless, she turned to the Levirate Law. In those days, since women were basically considered family property, this law arranged for the widows to be given in marriage to a brother-in-law if there was one. This arrangement increased the ability for the family line to continue. While established later in written form under the Law of Moses (see Deut. 25:5-10), this law pertinent to marriage was apparently a common practice long before. While its origin isn't known, according to most scholars, there have been some who believe it was a common social practice that was established to incur social and economic order. That is obviously a sensible assessment, since this is what was automatically put into practice in the case of Tamar.

Therefore, at the command of her father-in-law Judah, Tamar was able to marry Judah's second son, Onan. However, she now faced a new challenge with this husband, Onan, the brother of her deceased husband, Er. Onan didn't like this marriage arrangement because he knew the child would actually be considered his deceased brother's child and wouldn't truly be his own. He rebelled against it, causing him to come under the judgment of God like his brother Er. The anger of the Lord was because Onan refused to continue the family line even though he undoubtedly understood its importance as part of the family heritage in Abraham. This judgment against Onan caused him to die also, as he was refusing to offer his seed to continue this royal lineage that would bring forth the Breaker prophesied in Genesis 3:15.

Tamar's dream and breakthrough desire of having a child seemed lost. She had now been married twice and both husbands were dead and she still has no child. For a Jewish woman this meant disgrace because people thought being childless was a punishment from God. With unrelenting determination, she continued to expect this Levirate Law to be enforced in which she had a legal right to marry Judah's third son, Shelah. The only problem was she was now a much older widow than Judah's third son and therefore would have to wait until he is old enough to marry to bring forth a child. Judah saw his daughter-in-law, Tamar, as not being a good investment, since his two other sons died with her. He thought something was wrong with her, so he didn't want to endanger his last son, Shelah, by allowing him to marry her (see Gen. 38:11). Judah's solution was to send Tamar home to her father, which was humiliating in the culture of that time. He explained to her that she should remain there, as a widow, until the third son grew up; of course he was suggesting this with a deceptive motive. Time passed, and she was never able to marry Judah's third son, Shelah, because Judah never kept his promise to give her his son so she could have a child (see Gen. 38).

Maybe you have felt the same way as Tamar did—frustrated and feeling as though your breakthrough may never come. She desired a child, but the circumstances of life kept bringing more and more frustration. Still determined to have her rights respected and to have a child, she decided to trick Judah in a revengeful act of deception. She dressed up like a harlot, and carefully concealing her identity, went into town where she had heard that Judah would be passing by. Dressed as a harlot, she lured her father-in-law into having sexual relations with her. She did this because not only did she feel betrayed and lied to but because she wanted a child. Of course, she conceived and became pregnant. Sounds like a soap opera, doesn't it?

When it was time for Judah to pay Tamar as a harlot, he did not offer her money. Instead, he offered to send her a goat from his flock. Since he had to first leave to go fetch the goat, Tamar wanted something valuable of his to be left with her as a pledge that he would in fact return with payment. Intending to frame him, she talked him into leaving his tribal leader's staff, which was his personal seal. These items would have had his emblem or name carved on them. They were of great personal worth, and not only would she be sure he would return to get them, but they would also prove she had been with him.

Judah, seeking to make payment and regain his seal, sent his friend to pay this unknown prostitute for him, except when his friend got there, this harlot was nowhere to be found. Tamar had gone home without telling anyone who she was or what she had just done. She had become pregnant, achieving her goal of having a child by tricking her father-in-law, Judah. When others discovered she was pregnant and unmarried, she was taken to Judah her father-in-law for her disciplinary sentence, since she was considered his property. Judah immediately condemned her to death by burning (see Gen. 38:20-26).

Now three months pregnant, she showed Judah the staff, seal, and cord that he left with her. "These," she said, "belonged to the man by who I am with child." She then asked him to tell her whose name was written on them. Judah, confronted by the evidence, had no choice but to acknowledge that he had been wrong, and that she had been within the law. He admitted his sinful actions and that Tamar was more righteous than he was. This was because she had a legal right to have the inheritance of a child but was unjustly denied that right by not being given to Judah's next son, Shelah. Tamar was saved by her clever ploy, and as a result she bore twin boys from the seed of Judah, named Pharez and Zerah (see Gen. 38:27-30).

The happy ending to this story is that not only does Tamar give birth to these twins, but one of them, Pharez, becomes the direct ancestor of King

David. We find later that this is the lineage that eventually led to the Breaker, Jesus Christ!

She was a barrier breaker because she risked everything, her life and her reputation, to get what was rightfully hers, thereby obtaining her breakthrough. The birth of her sons was her reward. In other words, you could say that Tamar birthed her breakthrough!

Wrestling for Your Breakthrough

Like Tamar, you can birth your breakthrough also. We can see from this story of Tamar that she was desperate for her breakthrough. In spite of her methods, she was still taking what rightfully belonged to her, and God was able to operate through her barrier-breaking spirit. The Lord honored her faith in her lawful rights. Today, under the New Covenant in Christ, our methods for obtaining breakthrough are obviously held to a different moral standard that is depicted in the New Testament way of living. Jesus came teaching new methods for brotherly kindness, love, and morality that were very different from the Old Testament mind-set.

However, what we should mimic in Tamar is her breakthrough attitude that she wouldn't stop until her rightful promises were manifested. She held onto the promises in God's Word, under the Levirate Law, even after setback after setback. If you have experienced multiple setbacks after trying for your own breakthrough, let me encourage you not to give up hope. Tamar's determination led to one of the most amazing breakthroughs recorded in Scripture, but what if she had given up? She would have not been part of the family line that birthed Jesus Christ.

Then we see as her twins are born how this spirit of breakthrough continues. At the time of her delivery, it was as if there was a wrestling match in her womb. The breaker spirit would also be found in one of her twins. Look at Genesis 38:27-30:

> *And it came to pass in the time of her travail, that, behold, twins were in her womb. And it came to pass, when she travailed, that the one put out his*

hand: and the midwife took and bound upon his hand a scarlet thread, say-
ing, This came out first. And it came to pass, as he drew back his hand, that,
behold, his brother came out: and she said, How hast thou broken forth? This
breach be upon thee: therefore his name was called Pharez. And afterward
came out his brother, that had the scarlet thread upon his hand: and his name
was called Zarah.

Something happened during the birthing of her babies. One of the infants extended his arm through the birth canal, causing the midwife to grasp his outstretched hand. She tied a scarlet thread around his wrist, announcing, "This one came out first" (see verse 28). This was to establish the birthright inheritance of the firstborn child. Except, something unusual happened. The first baby suddenly drew his arm back, and his twin brother pushed through the birth canal in front of him and was born first! The baby who was supposed to be born second became the first born, thus claiming the inheritance! Throughout the history of the Israelites, both they and God put great importance on the firstborn, especially among sons. This is because the firstborn inherited a double share of inheritance.

It was as if there was a wrestling match between those babies over the right for the inheritance of the firstborn. It would seem as if the breakthrough spirit in the baby that pushed his way through must have seen his brother's hand and said, "No you don't, get back in here!" Thus he fought for the inheritance that he received, having his name also mentioned in the lineage of Jesus Christ first, ahead of his brother! God watched those who fought to bring forth the lineage of the Messiah.

Like Jacob over Esau, in the book of Genesis, and now a similar fight for the blessing between these two baby boys, God looks for those who will break through to obtain the inheritance.

This apparent wrestling match ended with their being named after their behaviors in the birth process. The one child who broke through ahead of his brother was named Pharez, which means "breakthrough." In Scripture sometimes his name is also spelled Perez or Phares. His name was given because of his pushiness in "breaking through" from the womb ahead of his brother! The name Pharez also means to "break forth" (see Gen. 38:29). His brother, who put his hand out first with the scarlet thread, was named Zerah.

This Womb Wrestling Federation (WWF) match between these boys in the womb, Zerah versus Pharez, reveals to us that there was a wrestling going on for the blessing. It also reveals that in order to fully receive your rightful blessings in life, you are going to have to possess a breakthrough spirit, like Pharez. When this breakthrough baby broke through, the midwife said a breach had taken place. What did this mean? When the midwife said that his birth created a breach or gap, she was saying that there was an opening created like when an army might crush through enemy fortress walls and leave a hole in their defenses. She was describing a warring spirit. We see this depicted clearly in the life of David.

In Second Samuel 5, God, the Lord of the breakthrough, brings a breakthrough victory for David. Second Samuel 5:20 says:

> *And David came to Baalperazim, and David smote them there, and said, The LORD hath broken forth upon mine enemies before me, as the breach of waters. Therefore he called the name of that place Baalperazim* [Lord of the breakthrough].

This victory was so powerful that David called the place Baal-perazim, meaning the "Lord of the breakthrough." The site of David's victory over the Philistines and the great destruction of their images is also called "Mount Perazim." The word *Peraz* or *Perizim* is the same word as the name Pharez, meaning "breakthrough." The root word for Perez or Pharez in the Hebrew is *parats*. We talked about the word in the previous chapter because it is where we get the word "breaker." This helps reveal just how prophetic Pharez's birth was and how it foretold the coming of the Breaker, Jesus, through his family line!

Like Pharez and King David and even Jacob when he took the birthright from Esau, this is the kind of breakthrough God looks for. God's breakthrough is like the breaking of waters through a dam. It is with a rushing, great power like when the Holy Spirit came as a rushing, mighty wind in Acts 2.

On the other side, there are many who don't have this kind of barrier-breaking spirit. Let's look back at Pharez's twin brother Zerah. Putting his hand out first was a picture of someone who just wants a handout or has a handout mentality. They want their firstborn rights but don't want to fight for them. They want breakthrough and expect to receive their rightful inheritance as they have their hand out, like Zerah did, wanting and expecting a blessing without any effort. There's nothing wrong with wanting blessings, but many never try to possess a barrier-breaking spirit that gets God's attention, or causes the Breaker to come and go before them. They want what seems like the easiest option with the least amount of effort, and usually want others to do the work for them to get their breakthrough. They prefer others to do things like pray for them, counsel them, and get a hold of God for them.

This baby's name, Zerah, means "east, sunrise, and sprout." His name also means "rising" and is derived from the Hebrew word *zerach* meaning "dawning." This too describes many Christians. They tend to always look for a new sunny day, or a break in the darkness of what they are facing. They want their blessings and want things to sprout forth for them. There is nothing wrong with that, because we should all want blessings and things to get better. However, the problem is that some are expecting it without having to do what it takes to manifest a breakthrough (Pharez) first! If we want breakthrough, it often requires work and dedication. It is the person who doesn't give up who gets the blessing! We have to be willing, like Pharez and Tamar, to wrestle and fight for our breakthrough with expectancy and determination.

The Determined Spirit

A spirit of expectancy and determination will get God's attention and cause Him to break through for us. This barrier breaker, Pharez, as we mentioned before, was from the lineage of Jacob, who was his grandfather. In order to really see the importance of this barrier breaker, we need to look more closely at the DNA that was passed down from his grandfather. Remember how he also took the birthright away from Esau (see Gen. 25:29-34)? From this, we will find that it represents breakthrough for those who are in Christ because this barrier breaker lineage that began with God the Father is passed down until Jesus is born. Those who are in Christ are now partakers of this breakthrough spirit as well, because they have now been made partakers of His divine Nature. Second Peter 1:4 says, *"Whereby are given unto us exceeding great and precious promises: that by these ye might be partakers of the divine nature..."* His divine nature is that of breakthrough, and that's why He chose to come from Heaven through an earthly lineage with that same spirit.

Like his grandson's birth, Jacob's birth was also prophetic concerning the Breaker (Jesus). The prophets kept prophesying that this Breaker was coming. The devil feared the words of the prophets concerning this and put many to death at the hand of religious and wicked people who despised the barrier-breaker spirit. As said before, if he knew the mystery of the Breaker, he wouldn't have crucified the Lord Jesus Christ.

God was looking for those, in the covenant He made with Abraham and his seed, who would carry this breakthrough spirit. Like the twins of Tamar, Jacob and Esau had a similar story. They too had a struggle in the womb at the time of their birth. Genesis 25:22-24 says:

> *And the children struggled together within her; and she said, If it be so, why am I thus? And she went to enquire of the LORD. And the LORD said unto her, Two nations are in thy womb, and two manner of people shall be separated from thy bowels; and the one people shall be stronger than the other people; and the elder shall serve the younger. And when her days to be delivered were fulfilled, behold, there were twins in her womb.*

This gives us an indication at just how serious the promise of the Breaker was and of the firstborn rights concerning it. We see in this womb a struggle between Jacob and Esau, another prophetic womb wrestling match for the inheritance just like the one with Zerah and Pharez. Notice how Jacob was born? He was born with a prophetic foreshadowing. Genesis 25:26 says, *"And after that came his brother out, and his hand took hold on Esau's heel; and his name was called Jacob...."*

This baby, Jacob, was showing us a prophetic truth by laying hold of his brother Esau's heel. He was leading the way for what his grandson Pharez would eventually do! He was showing a prophetic mystery of the Breaker and the barrier-breaking people called God's Church that would arise. We find a piece of this prophetic picture in the fact that Jacob grabbed the heel of his brother as he was being born. Why the heel? First, it was another reminder of the prophecy concerning the Breaker (Jesus) who was coming through the womb of a woman and how His *heel* would be used to crush the devil. Genesis 3:15 (NIV) says:

> And I will put enmity between you and the woman, and between your
> offspring and hers; he will crush your head, and you will strike his heel.

When Jacob grabbed his brother's heel, it was as if God was saying, "Because you have grabbed the heel of your brother, I, the Breaker, will now come through the linage of Jacob until it leads to the birth of my Son, the Breaker Jesus Christ, born through a virgin girl named Mary!" Again, God watched for the one who would grab a hold, fight for his or her rights, and possess a barrier-breaker spirit. He was looking for which child would position himself to continue the family lineage to bring forth the ultimate Breaker. We know that Jesus the Breaker completely crushed the head of the serpent and will do it again. Romans 16:20 (MSG) says:

> Stay alert like this, and before you know it the God of peace will come down
> on Satan with both feet, stomping him into the dirt.

Have you ever wondered why the Bible said that God loved Jacob and hated Esau? Malachi 1:2-3 says:

> I have loved you, saith the LORD. Yet ye say, Wherein hast Thou loved us?
> Was not Esau Jacob's brother? saith the LORD: yet I loved Jacob, and I
> hated Esau. . . .

It was because Jacob had the same determination that was shown in his birth to grab his brother's heel and gain the birthright that was foreshadowing the breaker spirit. Even though Jacob used deceit, like Tamar, to get his brother's birthright, it still led to God honoring it because Esau would rather satisfy his flesh with a bowl of soup than respect and fight for the birthright. Hebrews 12:16-17(NIV) says:

> *See that no one is sexually immoral, or is godless like Esau, who for a single meal sold his inheritance rights as the oldest son. Afterward, as you know, when he wanted to inherit this blessing, he was rejected. He could bring about no change of mind, though he sought the blessing with tears.*

The reason the Lord didn't honor Esau is because Esau didn't honor the birthright. After all, it would be this birthright that would continue and help bring the Breaker and the breaker spirit into the earth. Esau didn't respect that promise, so neither did God respect Esau. The Lord allowed it to be taken from him and given to Jacob, who had a determination. Again, I need to reiterate that like these Old Testament people, we aren't to defraud people to achieve our breakthroughs because Jesus, the ultimate Breaker, set a different standard. But we are to carry the spirit of breakthrough. If we are to possess this birthright and inheritance from the Breaker, Jesus, who we are joint heirs with, then we must rise up and take hold of what is rightfully ours by faith. Romans 8:16-17 says:

> *The Spirit itself beareth witness with our spirit, that we are the children of God: and if children, then heirs; heirs of God, and joint-heirs with Christ. . . .*

Just as Jacob grabbed his brother's heel, we need to grab hold of our inheritance that is in Christ our Lord and elder brother! Hebrews 2:11-12 (NIV) says:

> *Both the one who makes men holy and those who are made holy are of the same family. So Jesus is not ashamed to call them brothers. He says, "I will declare your name to My brothers; in the presence of the congregation I will sing your praises.*

This means we have, and must grab hold by faith, this same barrier-breaking spirit as Jacob and possess our inheritance that our elder brother, Jesus, has given us. We can't be like Esau and live our Christian lives wasting our inheritance and constantly satisfying our fleshly appetites, never rising up with a barrier-breaking spirit.

This wrestling, breakthrough nature in Jacob qualified him, in God's eyes, to carry on the lineage that would manifest the Breaker. God watched Jacob's birth as he later did with Pharez to see which child would possess a determination and breakthrough spirit, because that is what it takes to inherit the promises. Interestingly enough, it was Jacob who gave birth to the twelve tribes of Israel and continued the breakthrough spirit in Pharez and his descendents. This family lineage, as we said before, leads to the birth of Jesus Christ according to Matthew 1. Notice both Jacob and Pharez are mentioned, and look who is mentioned last in these verses. It is Jesus Christ, who is also the fulfillment of the prophetic seed of Genesis 3:15!

Look at Matthew 1:2-6,16 (MSG):

> *Abraham had Isaac, Isaac had Jacob, Jacob had Judah and his brothers, Judah had Perez and Zerah (the mother was Tamar), Perez had Hezron, Hezron had Aram, Aram had Amminadab, Amminadab had Nahshon, Nahshon had Salmon, Salmon had Boaz (his mother was Rahab), Boaz had Obed (Ruth was the mother), Obed had Jesse, Jesse had David, and David became king. David had Solomon (Uriah's wife was the mother), Solomon had Rehoboam..., Jacob had Joseph, Mary's husband, the Mary who gave birth to Jesus, the Jesus who was called Christ.*

Not only was the breaker spirit in Jacob as he grabbed the heel of his brother but also when he was older and wrestled for his blessing at Bethel.

> *And Jacob was left alone; and there wrestled a man with him until the breaking of the day. And when he saw that he prevailed not against him, he touched the hollow of his thigh; and the hollow of Jacob's thigh was out of joint, as he wrestled with him. And he said, Let me go, for the day breaketh.*

And he said, I will not let thee go, except thou bless me. And he said unto him, What is thy name? And he said, Jacob (Gen. 32:24-27).

In this account with Jacob, he had to wrestle for his breakthrough in order for his blessing to come afterward. Again, this is the same spirit imparted in the DNA of Jacob's son, Judah. Further in this book we will look more closely at how the name Judah means praise in the Hebrew. Praise is important if we are going to enjoy a life of breakthrough. It was Judah and his tribe who were to go first into battle to break open and break through so that the battle would surely be won! Praise creates a breach or gap in the enemy's defenses.

This breaker spirit that was prophesied to come as a serpent crusher came from the seed of Jacob, to his son Judah, and it continued in Tamar and Judah's son, Pharez, but it didn't stop there! The Bible says that King David appointed chief warriors who had this same breaker spirit. One of his chief warriors came from the family line of Pharez. First Chronicles 27:3 says, *"Of the children of Perez was the chief of all the captains of the host for the first month."* He had many descendants from his blood line who were barrier breakers and valiant men. Nehemiah 11:6 says, *"All the sons of Perez* [Pharez] *that dwelt at Jerusalem were four hundred threescore and eight valiant men."* No wonder God chose Jacob and Pharez!

This sheds some interesting light on the Breaker coming to break through for the remnant of Israel, like the sheep of Bozrah discussed in chapter 2. Notice God said He would assemble the remnant of Jacob. The reason for this is because of their barrier-breaking spirit God was developing and the prom-ised Breaker that was coming. The king was coming to break through for them, and together they would break through with Jesus, the Breaker. Let's look again at a verse we read in chapter 2.

"I will surely assemble, O Jacob, all of thee; I will surely gather the remnant of Israel; I will put them together as the sheep of Bozrah, as the flock in the midst of their fold: they shall make great noise by reason of the multitude of men. The breaker is come up before them: they have broken up, and have passed through the gate, and are gone out by it: and their king shall pass before them, and the LORD on the head of them" (Micah 2:12-13).

This breaker spirit of a "no-quit" attitude in Jacob, Tamar, and Pharez is also found in many of their descendants. Let's look at a few examples of Pharez and his descendants in Scripture:

- Pharez (Phares/Perez): his name means "breakthrough, breach, bursting forth."

- It was from Pharez that the royal line of David came (see Ruth 4:12, 18-22).

- Pharez's descendants were the chief of all the captains of the host of the armies of David (see 1 Chron. 27:3).

- Four hundred and sixty-eight of his Pharez's "sons," meaning descendants, came back from captivity with Zerubbabel. Zerubbabel was also a descendent of Judah and Pharez (see 1 Chron. 9:4, Matt. 1).

- Pharez is listed in the genealogy of Jesus Christ (see Matt. 1:3; Luke 3:33).

When the Bible speaks of the descendents of Pharez, it is also in the context of the same breakthrough spirit. The reason again that God chose Jacob and Pharez was because of their breakthrough spirit.

Even though the heel-grabbing baby named Jacob and the breakthrough baby, Pharez, both displayed a breaker spirit that God was looking for, it doesn't imply that Zerah or Esau were bad babies or did anything wrong. After all, they were just babies. However, what they do represent is something that often indicates what kind of spirit we first possess when we approach problems, since birth speaks of beginnings. Esau and Zerah represent those who don't initially react with breakthrough when the opportunity is before them.

Looking for a Handout

Like Zerah, every one of us has to resist the temptation of coming to God with our hand out while lacking a breakthrough spirit. This kind of mentality for many is a first response. First responses can be very important because they are like seeds: once planted, seeds progress. When a problem arises in your life, you can just lie back and cry, hoping something will work out, or you can fight back. Many miss out because they don't fight back.

This kind of mentality reminds me of when I went out for wrestling in my younger years. I was wrestling against a kid who wouldn't wrestle back. My opponent seemed so scared and just laid on the mat while I tried to put different wrestling holds on him. All the while the coach and the rest of the team were yelling, "Come on, do something, you fish!" This was a phrase used in reference to any opponent who didn't do anything to wrestle back but just flapped like a fish. They were comparing my opponent to the natural way a fish reacts when it's out of water. The fish lays on the ground unable to do anything, no offensive weapons, and just flaps a lot. This described my opponent perfectly. I won the match because my opponent wasn't determined to wrestle back and didn't have the fight in him to win.

This is the wrestling mind-set of many who spiritually want blessings and breakthrough. They continue to let their adversary, the devil, mess with them while they do nothing in return, except maybe a little flapping reaction, while all the hordes of hell are yelling and mocking, "Do something you fish (or sheep)!" Then you have others who expect and want blessings but just give up in fear like my wrestling opponent. They sign up for the team of Christianity expecting to be a barrier breaker and have breakthrough blessings, except they are fearful or too lazy to rise up and do anything. They expect things to be handed to them because they are on the team, but they are either intimidated by their challenge or unwilling to work for it. Remember, if you want to be a barrier breaker, it will require effort, determination, and work.

Zerah putting his hand out during birth seems like a small, insignificant thing, doesn't it? However, to God it wasn't, because it disqualified Zerah from the birthright of the firstborn. We know this as his name is mentioned after Pharez in the lineage that brought forth Jesus, and Pharez's descendants are mentioned after his name but Zerah's descendants are not mentioned. Matthew 1:3 (NIV) says, *"Judah the father of Perez and Zerah, whose mother was Tamar, Perez the father of Hezron, Hezron the father of Ram..."* It also speaks to us, prophetically, of a determined spirit and mind-set that is lacking in many Christians. This is why

I refer to it as "Zerah-type" Christians. These are Christians who, similar to Zerah, like to stick their hands out and most always have some kind of need. They live their lives for what is in it for them and are always looking for a hand-out. Zerah-type Christians don't want to work for their breakthrough. Instead they are always putting their hands out expecting others to help and bless them. It is what could be called a beggar's mentality, since they expect blessings without working for them. This kind of spirit and mentality has hurt a lot of churches that are trying to build and advance the Kingdom. These Zerah-type Christians come to church looking for what they can get or receive, instead of what they can give. They don't give anything in return to the vision but are constantly taking from it by not tithing, giving, serving; they are uncommitted and always seeking for the pastor's time, continually looking for their blessing.

Many times I have had people who want me to invest so much into them and bless them, prophesy to them, pray for them, and serve them. However, they do nothing or very little to show that they intend to bless anyone in return.

This kind of Zerah mentality is often with a fleshly motivation and way of living. They don't consider being a barrier breaker or helping others to break through. Instead they seek for attention and hoard up their own blessings. We can see how true this is and how prevalent it really is in many churches by looking at the percentage of people who attend prayer meetings versus the percentage of those who come for some social gatherings in the church. The numbers are dramatically smaller in prayer and always higher in the gratifying of the flesh. Worse yet, many churches don't have prayer as a priority because of the lack of commitment. This is mostly because of a self-seeking, handout mentality in these Zerah-type Christians. This fleshly handout behavior is often with selfish motives and can even lead to compromise.

This is what happened with the descendants of Zerah. Zerah started a line of people who didn't help and support Israel, but they too had their hand out. The end result was that many suffered in the camp of Israel because of it. We can see this in the story of a man named Achan. Not surprisingly, we will see here that he was in fact a descendant of Zerah. Joshua 6:18 says:

And ye, in any wise keep yourselves from the accursed thing, lest ye make yourselves accursed, when ye take of the accursed thing, and make the camp of Israel a curse, and trouble it.

It was because of Achan that the whole camp suffered. He put his hand out and took something that God said was accursed. Joshua 7:1 says:

For Achan, the son of Carmi, the son of Zabdi, the son of Zerah, of the tribe of Judah, took of the accursed thing: and the anger of the LORD was kindled against the children of Israel.

God told Joshua and Israel not to take the accursed thing after the attack on Jericho, but Achan didn't listen. The great grandson of Zerah had his hand out. In both cases, it speaks of those who always have their hand out, not for godly reasons but to satisfy their flesh like Esau. This also speaks of the characteristic of Christians who possess the mentality and spirit of compromise and fleshy behavior.

It is not hard to see the difference between Zerah's generations and Pharez's. The breakthrough child, Pharez, has blessing in his generations that have many barrier breakers who continue the generations to David (see Ruth 4:18). However, in Zerah's generations you find his great-grandson Achan, the thief, putting his hand out like his great-grandfather Zerah, and both are cut off from the Lord!

Handout Mentality or Breakthrough Spirit?

What can we learn from Zerah and Pharez? We can learn that we too have a wrestling that goes on inside of every one of us. It is the wrestling of our flesh versus the spirit; right from wrong; and either a breakthrough spirit or a passive one. We all have to choose to have a breakthrough spirit and resist a handout, codependent, depressed, feel-sorry-for-ourselves mentality, especially when it doesn't look like we are receiving answers to prayers or receiving a breakthrough from the Lord. It is not the handout mentality, like Zerah, that usually receives a breakthrough. It is those who refuse to quit, like Pharez.

Those who fight, forging through for breakthrough, get the Lord's attention! It was Pharez and Jacob, because of their breakthrough, determined spirit, who got God's attention and ultimately the greater blessing. We shouldn't expect to receive blessing or breakthrough if we are living in compromise like Achan. Proverbs 28:13 says, *"He that covereth his sins shall not prosper: but whoso confesseth and forsaketh them shall have mercy."*

The reason many become Zerah-type Christians is because their first response is usually that of a personal handout. They put their hands out first, as they would rather be served than to serve, and they would rather receive than give. But Jesus teaches that it is better to give than to receive (see Acts 20:35)! Too many people have developed a mentality and response to constantly put their hands out wanting blessings, yet they do nothing to create a breakthrough or even consider producing a breakthrough for themselves, let alone anyone else.

There are even Zerah-type churches full of these Zerah-type Christians. They are trying so hard to be relevant and trendy to keep the blessing of numbers, church members, but they possess no power to heal the sick, cast out devils, or preach the Kingdom. The Zerah church mentality makes churches so non-offensive, politically correct, "bless me," and "make me feel good" minded. Zerah-type Christians have their pastors wrapped around their fingers like the scarlet thread on the hand of Zerah! If they don't get their way, they will pout, rebel, or leave the church.

The Zerah spirit is often so codependent, pastoral-dependent, with a "my needs" mentality that it usually becomes totally dependant on others to help them break through. They never learn the skill to break through for themselves. There is certainly nothing wrong with seeking the wisdom of a pastor or asking prayer, but this can't always be the norm. This mentality can prove costly, especially in time of need, if you don't have anyone around but you to help you break through. You must remember that you possess the Pharez-type spirit because of Jesus Christ who is from that earthly lineage and has adopted you into the heavenly family lineage. His seed is in you. If Jesus is in you, then you possess the breakthrough spirit and ability to break through.

When I was first starting in the ministry, I was employed as a pastor at a local church. One day, I was assigned as the "pastor of the day," which meant you were to be the pastor on hand for people's unexpected needs that might arise. That day a stranger showed up at the church wanting money. I told him that I had no problem helping him with his needs. He said he needed money to buy a bus ticket to travel to another city. He professed to be a Christian and had fallen on hard times. However, something just didn't seem right. I felt in my heart he was lying and just wanted money to aid his many apparent problems and addictions that he didn't want to deal with. So, I decided to test him by asking him to give me one day of work since it was several hundred dollars he was asking for.

Do you know how he responded? He became very angry with me and began cussing and calling me all kinds of names. He was acting very different from the guy who professed to be a Christian just down on his "luck." He carried on, refusing to give any type of help around the church, and walked angrily away while giving me a not-so-nice hand gesture. All that was asked of him was for a few hours of work, like mowing the church lawn and doing some minor cleaning. This guy was not elderly or disabled either but very able-bodied to carry out the tasks. He didn't want to work for his blessing or breakthrough; instead he wanted a handout. Unfortunately, this is the same mentality of the spirit of Zerah that we are referring to.

The Bible gives us another glimpse of this Zerah Christian mentality with a man at a gate called Beautiful in Acts 3. He was looking for a handout rather than expecting a breakthrough.

> *And a certain man lame from his mother's womb was carried, whom they laid daily at the gate of the temple which is called Beautiful, to ask alms of them that entered into the temple...* (Acts 3:3-5).

This man who was lame and begging at the gate was looking for a handout rather than his breakthrough. How do we know this? Because he was asking for alms, and the Bible says he was looking for a handout. Acts 3:1-5 (MSG) says:

When he saw Peter and John about to enter the Temple, he asked for a hand-out. Peter, with John at his side, looked him straight in the eye and said, "Look here." He looked up, expecting to get something from them.

This verse says clearly that he was expecting to receive some money from Peter and John. This beggar had the Zerah mentality. He was expecting a hand-out rather than recognizing the opportunity of a lasting breakthrough. This could be because of mind-sets that were developed based on a daily routine. Remember, he was carried daily and set down at the temple gate. This is what could have formed his daily mentality of handouts rather than a breakthrough. This is where many can get caught up in the danger and trap to becoming passive or developing a beggar, Zerah way of life. This man's greatest need wasn't money, but his mind-sets and daily habits kept him from expecting anything else. What he needed was the anointing that Peter and John carried from the Holy Spirit. Peter was discerning enough not to let him accept this Zerah mind-set, but helped him to get his focus on the right thing. This is a necessary step if you want to position yourself for breakthrough. You must be willing to come out from the daily routines and mind-sets that can hinder you from having a true breakthrough spirit and mentality. Peter recognized his greatest need was not a handout that keeps the man the same, but instead a breakthrough that changes him forever!

Then Peter said, Silver and gold have I none; but such as I have give I thee: In the name of Jesus Christ of Nazareth rise up and walk (Acts 3:6).

Many, especially men, are like this man at the gate called Beautiful, spiritually speaking. They are begging outside the church and never breaking through with a breaker spirit. We often see more women with a breaker, determined spirit in the things of God. They often lead most of the prayer, worship, and zeal for the Lord in churches, more so than men. There is nothing wrong with women doing those things, but what it reveals is a spiritual beggar spirit that has bound many men. It is keeping them spiritually lame and from rising up with the breaker spirit.

This is why I believe the first recorded miracle after Pentecost was of a lame man walking and not a woman (see Acts 3:1-6). Because some men, like this man who was begging, have a "what's in it for me" mentality. For others it is the drive to have silver and gold that causes many men to have a beggar handout spirit and become spiritually lame. It is because they are always looking to make money and work, work, work, and they don't prioritize God or the church. Then if they do come, they hardly show any dedication, zeal, leadership, or expression to the Lord. They would rather have silver and gold and the riches of this world than a breakthrough spirit.

This man at gate Beautiful went into the temple leaping, dancing, praising God. This is the manifestation of one who receives breakthrough and continues to walk in it. Acts 3:7-9 says:

> *Immediately his feet and ankle bones received strength. And he leaping up stood, and walked, and entered with them into the temple, walking, and leaping, and praising God. And all the people saw him walking and praising God.*

This kind of mentality keeps a lot of people from receiving from the Lord. When I was first saved, I decided I was going to do what the Scripture said and evangelize. I was going to go out into the highways and byways of Omaha and invite someone to come to church with me. "There he is," I thought as I saw a homeless looking man on the side of the street sitting on a bench. "I will bring that man to church," I said. He had old, smelly, tattered clothes, and the smell of alcohol reeked on him so much that he smelled like a brewery.

I told him I wanted to bring him to church and would get him a meal. I knew he wasn't really interested in going to church but wanted a meal and to be in a warmer place. So, without talking much, he decided to go with me. Happy that I was doing my Christian duty, I brought this man to the church service. I walked him proudly down the first few rows of the front of this church that could seat upwards of a thousand people. He was fidgety, but at least he was behaving himself. Of course the whole front part of the church smelled so bad because of him, but hey, we are to love the unlovely.

Things were going along pretty well until it was communion time and it was real quiet in the church. My guest started sleeping and he began to snore so loud you could hear it echoing across the sanctuary. I think it was magnified by the microphones because we were sitting up front. After hearing some snickers and seeing people giving both of us the evil eye, I thought, "What am I going to do now?" I decided that I would just bump him lightly with my arm to wake him. Wrong decision! To my surprise, he immediately jumped up and yelled, "I am not sleeping, I am praying!" He wasn't praying at all. He was sleeping. I will never forget that moment of embarrassment. You know, he wasn't looking for a breakthrough to better his life and get saved and some help. He was looking for the Zerah-type handout of continuing his lifestyle without the attitude or decision for change. His handout and daily mentality outweighed his desire and determination to have a lifelong breakthrough!

Unfortunately, not everything in life is handed to us easy. That line of thinking is the Zerah spirit and mentality. This is why we need to possess a barrier-breaking spirit that rises up and works for it.

The Breakthrough Spirit

The kind of spirit that God wants to develop and wants us to possess is that of a breaker spirit. We can see from the examples in this chapter how important a breakthrough spirit is. We must be willing, at times, to wrestle for our blessing until it comes and grab our inheritance like Jacob when he wrestled for his breakthrough and grabbed his brother's heel at birth. We also saw how having a determined breakthrough spirit like Pharez will lead to a life of breakthrough.

While we do have to work our breakthrough and keep a breakthrough attitude through life, we also need to realize that in that process breakthrough can happen suddenly. It can happen suddenly and unexpectedly. This happened with Pharez too. His birth and the way he came out in front of his brother was unexpected and caught everyone by surprise. Yet, there was another dimension that made his breakthrough so powerful. His conception was surrounded in tragic circumstances, which could have been all the more a reason for him not to be a barrier breaker. The message for us is that something good can come out of something tragic. These types of "Pharez breakthroughs" are when a blessing comes unexpectedly in the middle of something that is impossible or tragic.

Yet, we still need to be people who work our breakthroughs of life, but be expectant that the sudden moment will come. We prepare for sudden break-throughs by a life of prayer. It comes as we labor in the Word of God and prayer until we give birth to our breakthrough. Just like giving birth to a natural baby, it is a process that requires labor, which affects each one quite differently, with different results. This is also how it is when birthing and laboring for a spiritual breakthrough. However, the bottom line is that we don't give up until the baby is born. We must never quit or stop because we are frustrated. We must continue to labor in prayer concerning what we are asking God to do for us.

This is how Pharez was born and how Pharez breakthroughs come that release sudden blessings. We mentioned in Chapter 2 that breakthroughs are usually progressive. Yet, the actual manifestation of breakthrough is usually immediate. It is what the Bible refers to in the King James Version as *straightway*, meaning "immediate." I believe we are in the season of "straightways" in the Body of Christ today. Look at some of the examples of the sudden, unexpected breakthroughs, the "straightways," of God! They all speak and reveal the spirit of breakthrough!

1. **God's going to suddenly come to His Church!**

    Behold, I will send My messenger, and He shall prepare the way before Me: and the LORD, whom ye seek, shall suddenly come to His temple, even the messenger of the covenant, whom ye delight in: behold, He shall come, saith the LORD of hosts (Malachi 3:1).

2. **The Holy Spirit comes with the Spirit of the Breaker!**

    And suddenly there came a sound from heaven as of a rushing mighty wind. . . (Acts 2:2).

3. Your problems or issues suddenly stop!

And a certain woman, which had an issue of blood twelve years, and had suffered many things of many physicians, and had spent all that she had, and was nothing bettered, but rather grew worse, when she had heard of Jesus, came in the press behind, and touched his garment. For she said, If I may touch but his clothes, I shall be whole. And straightway the fountain of her blood was dried up; and she felt in her body that she was healed of that plague (Mark 5:25-29).

4. Suddenly you become free from sin! (Leprosy is prophetic for a type of sin.)

And Jesus put forth His hand, and touched him, saying, I will; be thou clean. And immediately his leprosy was cleansed (Matthew 8:3).

5. You are healed suddenly from sickness and disease!

And a woman was there who had been subject to bleeding for twelve years, but no one could heal her. She came up behind Him and touched the edge of His cloak, and immediately her bleeding stopped (Luke 8:43-44 NIV).

Remember the very nature of a Pharez breakthrough. Sure, there may be a process leading up to it, but they can arrive unexpectedly and suddenly breakthrough comes. They catch us completely by surprise. Yet, for days and months like the womb of Tamar it is collimating, growing, and progressing until it suddenly breaks through!

This kind of breakthrough spirit is what Jesus carried when He walked this earth. He carried this breaker spirit, because He is the Breaker! His earthly lineage was from breakers such as Tamar, Jacob, Judah, and Pharez. His heavenly lineage is that He is the Son of God. Jesus, both in Heaven and earth, carries and manifests this breakthrough spirit. We see this on earth by how Jesus prayed! He prayed strong prayers and in the Garden of Gethsemane prayed so strong that He sweat drops of blood (see Heb. 5:7, Luke 22:44).

Everywhere Jesus went and whatever He did, He had breakthroughs, except in one account that we read in Scripture. He didn't have a breakthrough like He would have wanted. The Bible said He could do no mighty works because of the people's unbelief, except a few sick people were healed (see Mark 6:5). Sure, some received some blessings, but it didn't produce a breakthrough with greater results. That is the difference between handouts and breakthroughs. The Bible said there were only a few healed because of their unbelief. This spirit of unbelief is dangerous because it keeps us passive and renders us ineffective in our progression for breakthrough.

When it looks like nothing is happening, it is easy to want to quit or think nothing is happening. In the story of Daniel, we know that the Bible says the first day that he prayed the angel came for his prayers (see Dan. 10:8-13). It wasn't until 21 days later that the breakthrough manifested. Daniel needed to keep praying, believing, and standing for his breakthrough blessings. Let me encourage you to keep speaking God's Word and promises. Continue to be faithful in prayer and fight for your inheritance rights that are yours in Christ! It is part of the ingredients that lead to a breakthrough when you refuse to quit. This is vital because, like with Daniel, your breakthrough may be right at your door. It just needs you to grab hold of it and refuse to let go until your breakthrough comes!

Chapter Four

BIRTHING YOUR BREAKTHROUGH MOMENT

And the angel said unto her, Fear not, Mary: for thou hast found favour with God. and, behold, thou shalt conceive in thy womb, and bring forth a son, and shalt call His name JESUS. He shall be great, and shall be called the Son of the Highest: and the Lord God shall give unto Him the throne of His father David: And He shall reign over the house of Jacob for ever; and of His kingdom there shall be no end (Luke 1:30-33).

A baby born in a feeding trough? What good could come from a mere feeding trough? To the world and the innkeeper on duty that night, nothing seemed out of the ordinary or very significant at all. Everything appeared normal, except a man and his pregnant wife in need of a place to stay. Settling for a barn fit for livestock, this family retired for the night, waiting for the fullness of time to come. Something that night was about to break through in the earth! It was coming from the womb of this woman pregnant with child and pregnant with destiny. All seemed normal in this town like any other night, in the place where they were staying, except for the birth about to take place. You could hear the sounds of this newborn baby that night breaking through into the earth. The cries sounded like any other newborn cry, yet these cries were different because they echoed throughout the heavens, hell, and the earth! They were no ordinary cries but cries that were declaring that salvation, deliverance, and breakthrough had come.

They were abnormal surroundings for a baby's birth, but this would prove to be no ordinary child. Yet still, if there was really anything important about this baby, certainly there would be a special room made for such a one in the town inn, right?

Who is this child? The night seemed insignificant, but something long awaited was taking place. Yet, the world carried on as normal, as if no one significant was being born or any grand event was happening. However, history was being birthed, and the greatest child ever born of a woman was now entering the world, but the world knew Him not. The world was oblivious to such a grand event and seemingly insignificant birth, but it was time for what the prophets had spoken for centuries to now come. It was time for the Breaker, the Serpent Crusher to be born and fulfill Genesis 3:15.

It was not just this woman's natural birthing but a breakthrough had come for all people! It was as the angels declared, "Peace on earth, good will toward men." The Lord had come to earth to break through so He could rescue humankind who had been lost. Yet, only a few could see past this seemingly insignificant moment in order to see that a breakthrough had come for humanity. It was the birth of the Breaker, Jesus Christ, the Savior of the world. He had finally come.

That night when angels gathered to announce His seemingly lowly birth to a few shepherds, the majority of people had no clue as to what had just happened. It is the same way today for many and is often why they don't receive their breakthrough! It is because they don't expect anything miraculous to ever happen or they ignore all the signs that a breakthrough is in process. Then there are some who quit because it seems the promise of breakthrough is delayed and will never come. For others they are too busy with things in this earth, so they never prepare themselves for a spiritual breakthrough to invade Earth.

This is often the reaction to many who either don't discern what they are carrying inside of them or their potential for greatness and breakthrough. This is because we often don't realize the opportunity we have been given in Christ to birth greatness. Mary was a young, ordinary woman who was chosen by God to give birth to something great. What do I mean by giving birth? I am speaking of course about your life, your decisions, and your potential to bring your dreams and desires to fruition. Many don't realize that they are pregnant with promises, dreams, a purpose, and great opportunities. There are so many things in this life to challenge us, resist us, and discourage us, and are meant to try and abort what we are pregnant with. This is all meant to stop our desire for breakthrough and force us to just give up.

Mary had to cooperate with God's plan concerning her and believe that what He said He would do. She did this by being faithful to God and believing His word. She obeyed the Lord by refusing to doubt or quit in difficult times. Mary had to carry her breakthrough until the time of birthing. She had to be part of a progression and a process that would bring her breakthrough forth.

This was not just a breakthrough moment that would affect only her, but all generations forever. Remember, Mary was pregnant with breakthrough, and so are you.

Birthing Your Breakthrough Moment!

We can receive our breakthrough promise just as Mary did because who she birthed still affects those today who are Christians. The reason is because if you are a Christian, then you have the same Breaker, the Lord Jesus Christ, in you, *"...which is Christ in you, the hope of glory"* (Col. 1:27). That means, just like Mary did in the natural, you can spiritually birth your breakthrough moment with the help of the Breaker, the Lord.

Mary was pregnant with breakthrough, the Breaker Himself. This is why we have read in previous chapters of this book the family progression that led to Mary's birth. We found that Abraham, Jacob, Tamar, Judah, Pharez, and David, to name a few, are those with a determined spirit of breakthrough. The Lord's nature is so much of a Breaker, that He wanted those in the earth who would carry His same spirit. This is why God chose in this family lineage one baby, at different times, over the other as we saw with Jacob and Esau or Pharez and Zerah. This was to protect and develop the breaker lineage from which he

Himself would be born in the earth. This is why God chose Mary, because she too had this spirit of a barrier breaker and God knew it and chose her! He knew she would obey Him and trust His word and be determined to bring her breakthrough moment to fruition. He also chose Joseph, her husband and Jesus' earthly father, because he also possessed this same spirit. He helped to aid God by obeying the Lord every step of the way in the process, even when it meant his reputation would be questioned. He could have quit and refused to have anything to do with this child who was by the Holy Spirit and not by him. God saw a breaker spirit in Joseph that would obey God's instructions that came through a few dreams and visitations from God.

The birthing process through Mary revealed that God had found two barrier breakers in Mary and Joseph. This is why the event that night was not insignificant, as it may have seemed. Not only did it bring out the barrier breaker spirit in Mary and Joseph, but Jesus was also born, and He brings out the barrier breaker spirit in us. We now have been adopted into His family when we are born again and now posses that breaker spirit through Him! We are part of a heavenly lineage of barrier breakers.

> *He predestined us to be adopted as his sons through Jesus Christ, in accordance with His pleasure and will* (Ephesians 1:5 NIV).

This means we have the same breaker spirit as Jesus, because He lives in us and we have been adopted as sons and daughters by our Heavenly Father. We have also inherited those same blessings as Abraham and his lineage. We are now called the sons of Abraham, entitled to the same breaker spirit that they had naturally and also spiritually because of our heavenly adoption in Christ.

> *Ye are the children of the prophets, and of the covenant which God made with our fathers, saying unto Abraham, And in thy seed shall all the kindreds of the earth be blessed* (Acts 3:25).

This verse tells us that because of Abraham, all people of the earth have the right to the blessing given to him. So we have earthly and heavenly blessing and potential for breakthrough. The Scripture declares that Abraham is the father of us all. This means we are entitled to the same blessing and break-through promise to him because of our heavenly lineage in Christ.

> *...But to that also which is of the faith of Abraham; who is the father of us all...* (Romans 4:16).

> *Know ye therefore that they which are of faith, the same are the children of Abraham* (Galatians 3:7).

It is because we, as Christians, belong to Christ that we are now entitled to those same blessings that were given to Abraham.

> *And if you belong to Christ, then you are Abraham's descendants, heirs according to promise* (Galatians 3:29 NASB).

When we are born again, our spiritual birth is significant for breakthrough as well, just like Mary's birthing of Jesus, because we give birth to a life in Christ. This is why the Bible tells us that Jesus in us is greater than he that is in the world, the devil (see 1 John 4:4). We have Jesus living inside us and we are born again of the same spirit so we don't have to fail. We can experience break-through after breakthrough. Don't you see just how much you have stacked in your favor to succeed, now that you have Christ the Breaker in you?

We can learn so much from Mary's example of birthing Jesus Christ, the Breaker. We can apply the things Mary did to our lives in order to birth our own breakthrough moment. What did she do to prepare herself? Let's look at a few things that we find in Scripture that she did to bring her breakthrough into the earth. If we apply these principles and align ourselves with them, with the Lord at our side, we only better position ourselves for a breakthrough moment.

- **She had the Holy Ghost—(breakthrough needs the Holy Ghost)**

> *Now the birth of Jesus Christ was on this wise: when as His mother Mary was espoused to Joseph, before they came together, she was found with child of the Holy Ghost* (Matthew 1:18).

- She was pure, a virgin—(breakthrough needs purity)

  "The virgin will be with child and will give birth to a son" (Matthew 1:23 NIV).

- She had God's intervention—(breakthrough needs God's help)

  "...And they will call Him Immanuel" which means, "God with us" (Matthew 1:23).

- She was connected to a father of her breakthrough and spiritual fathers—(breakthrough needs the "father" of the House)

  But he did not have sexual relations with her until her son was born. And Joseph named Him Jesus (Matthew 1:25 NLT).

- She understood the power of worship—(breakthrough needs the worship and honor to God)

  And when they were come into the house, they saw the young child with Mary His mother, and fell down, and worshipped Him: and when they had opened their treasures, they presented unto Him gifts; gold, and frankincense and myrrh (Matthew 2:11).

- She believed God and His word—(breakthrough needs to believe and trust the Word of God)

  For with God nothing shall be impossible (Luke 1:37).

- She obeyed God's word and submitted her will—(breakthrough holds onto the promise and doesn't quit)

  And Mary said, Behold the handmaid of the Lord; be it unto me according to Thy word (Luke 1:38).

Grace Needed for Breakthrough

Mary continued to be faithful with the process of birthing her breakthrough moment and thus positioned herself for blessing. There was something happening that would also change the course of history, helping to bring the Breaker forth. It was taking place in the womb of Mary's cousin Elizabeth.

She was also pregnant with a child of destiny, who would be born six months before Mary's child.

> *"And did you know that your cousin Elizabeth conceived a son, old as she is? Everyone called her barren, and here she is six months pregnant! Nothing, you see, is impossible with God"* (Luke 1:36-38 MSG).

The baby inside Elizabeth was conceived and born first, ahead of Mary's child, for a purpose. It reveals to those of us who need a breakthrough a powerful principle that we will discover concerning grace and how it is necessary for breakthrough. It is important to note that Elizabeth and her husband Zechariah were a lot older then Mary, and the Bible says they were stricken in years.

> *And Zacharias said unto the angel, Whereby shall I know this? for I am an old man, and my wife well stricken in years* (Luke 1:18).

This is good news for you and me. It means we are never too old to birth our breakthrough moment and we are never too old to be a barrier breaker. Their prayers were answered, and they were about to experience their own breakthrough.

> *But the angel said unto him, Fear not, Zacharias: for thy prayer is heard; and thy wife Elisabeth shall bear thee a son, and thou shalt call his name John* (Luke 1:13).

What does the birth of the child born to Elizabeth and her husband Zachariah signify to us today? This child, like Mary's, would not be an ordinary birth either but an extraordinary birth that would prepare the way for the ultimate breakthrough. We know that ultimate breakthrough was Jesus coming to this earth to bring victory to humankind. The birth of Elizabeth's child was to forerun the Breaker. Jesus later said of him that there was no greater prophet born of men. Of course, we know his name was John.

> *For I say unto you, Among those that are born of women there is not a greater prophet than John the Baptist...* (Luke 7:28).

Why was his birth so significant and why was it important for him to be born ahead of the Breaker? Some prophetic answers to this question are found again in the meaning of his name. His name, John, is pronounced *"Jahn."* It is of Hebrew origin and its meaning is "God's grace." His name also means grace in Greek as well.

You see, your breakthrough has a name and it is called *"John!"* What do I mean by this? The birth of John or Grace is to signify that it will take grace to have breakthrough. The very purpose and definition of his name gives us a prophetic ingredient for breakthrough. It is the element that helps to forerun or aid us in producing a breakthrough. You see, our breakthroughs often require a forerunning. John the Baptist was a forerunner for Jesus' ministry. Mark 1:2 says, *"Behold, I send My messenger before Thy face, which shall prepare Thy way before Thee."* John prepared the way for Jesus' ministry. To us today it means that we have to prepare because breakthrough is a process as we discussed in Chapter 2. Then it is like we said in Chapter 3 that it requires a determined, no-quit, and stand-on-God's-promise attitude.

Let's look at a list of things that helped to birth John the Baptist in the earth and see how it relates to us. These principles can be applied to help step into the kind of grace that brings breakthrough. Then we will look at a few more in depth to further help us tap into the grace we need.

- Be connected to a godly pastor, mentor, or spiritual parents—Luke 1:5

- Walk pure, holy, and blameless before God—Luke 1:6

- Don't give up no matter how long you have believed with little or no apparent results—Luke 1:7

- Rejoice and praise God for and over your breakthrough—Luke 1:14

- Speak rightly concerning your breakthrough, do not doubt—Luke 1:20

- Stay connected to God and the local church—Luke 1:21

- Prophesy to and about your breakthrough—Luke 1:67

All of these things brought John (grace) forth and will help you if you apply them to your life as well. Let's look now more in depth on some other things that happened leading up to John the Baptist's birth.

Identify your breakthrough need. It started with identifying the breakthrough that was necessary. It was a dark time in the earth at the time of Jesus' birth. Some Bible scholars conclude that it had been prophetically silent for 400 years from the time of Malachi to John the Baptist because no more books of Scripture were written. The announcement of the birth of John shattered that silent period and was a declaration that light was finally coming to pierce that darkness.

> *And the light shines in the darkness, and the darkness did not comprehend it. There was a man sent from God, whose name was John. This man came for a witness, to bear witness of the Light, that all through him might believe. He was not that Light, but was sent to bear witness of that Light* (John 1:5-8 NKJV).

The birth of these two babies, John and Jesus, simultaneously declared that God's grace and breakthrough were coming for the people.

Name your breakthrough! What is in a name? The naming of John was so important that God sent an angel to intervene in the naming of John. It is important to name and declare your breakthrough to aid you for your breakthrough moment. A name helps bring an identity to something. This is why it is helpful to study the meanings of names in Scripture because they often hold prophetic meanings significant to messages God wants us to receive (see Luke 1:59-60).

To name your breakthrough, you might declare or name your financial need as a provision miracle. Whenever you feel anxiety or worry concerning your financial need, you keep declaring what you named it. You can just start saying, "I declare provision, because the Word of God declares that God meets every one of my needs according to His riches and glory by Christ Jesus" (see Phil. 4:19).

Start with a seed! The next thing to consider, as we mentioned at the beginning of this book, would be to start with a seed. Breakthrough starts with a seed. Perhaps the seed you give would be in the form of a financial one, assuming that is the nature of the kind of breakthrough you need. Now, this doesn't mean that your seed always has to correspond with the type of breakthrough you need. For example, you can plant a financial seed even if you need a physical healing; you can still reap your breakthrough for healing, even though you gave a financial seed. The seed and the result don't match but still yield a breakthrough. This is because you put a spiritual law of reaping and sowing into practice (see Gal. 6:9).

Watch your words. One of the things that was important to birthing this child named grace (John) was the element of silence. Of course we need to speak and declare God's promises regarding our breakthrough, but we can't speak negatively. In John's example, God had to close his father Zachariah's mouth because he was speaking wrong over his breakthrough moment yet to manifest. So, God had the angel Gabriel close his mouth because he was speaking doubt, unbelief, or tradition.

> *The angel answered, "I am Gabriel. I stand in the presence of God, and I have been sent to speak to you and to tell you this good news. And now you will be silent and not able to speak until the day this happens, because you did not believe my words, which will come true at their proper time"* (Luke 1:19-20 NIV).

Traditionally, the child should have been named after or by the father pertinent to the family heritage. The name John wasn't in the family (see Luke 1:60-61). Zechariah was having a hard time with this, so the angel closed his mouth so his traditional hang-ups wouldn't disrupt the coming promise. That is because God knew that to birth breakthrough we would first need grace, so He made sure Zechariah would not hinder that element with his words.

We need to avoid speaking negatively about our needed breakthrough, especially in seasons when it looks like everything is the opposite or our own traditional minds are being challenged. This is where a lot of people miss their breakthrough moment. It has to do with their mouth. Often when walking through the process for our breakthrough, especially when it looks delayed, we have to be careful that we don't start speaking wrong because the events seem different than what we expect.

We really need to put self-control and discipline over our words. Zachariah and Elizabeth had to watch their words or possibly lose their breakthrough. This was especially true because they were old and it wasn't naturally possible to have children but only supernaturally possible. The best thing for them, and for you and I, is to watch our words. If we don't, then we can possibly lose our breakthrough moment or get into being double-minded. That is dangerous to our breakthrough because then it will keep us from receiving anything from God (see James 1:6-8).

Realize the power of Grace for breakthrough. When working or birthing your breakthrough, it is important to understand something you have available to aid you in your need. It is called Grace. This is why John's birth was ahead of Jesus. It is because you need grace to birth or forerun your miracle. Grace is simply God's unmerited favor. It is favor, help, privileges, or intervention you didn't expect, but God brought these things because He is gracious. I once heard grace defined as, *"I can't, therefore God must."* This grace, this unmerited favor, has already been given to us because Jesus has already made a way for us. We have grace so readily available right now, because we now have access to the throne room of God through the blood of Jesus.

> *Let us therefore come boldly unto the throne of grace, that we may obtain mercy, and find grace to help in time of need* (Hebrews 4:16).

We can now at the throne receive grace, mercy, and help in the time of need.

Prophesy your breakthrough. On the opposite end of speaking wrong concerning breakthrough, we also need to be sure we are speaking what is right. There is power when we declare, prophesy, and decree things. We can name circumstances. We learn this principle by looking at Genesis 2 when God had Adam name the animals. Genesis 2:19 says, *"And whatsoever Adam called every living creature, that was the name thereof.*" It was whatever Adam named the animals they would be called. The same principle is true today regarding the power of our words. What we speak out of our mouth we bring into manifestation, and it will be like with the animals named by Adam, exactly as we have named and prophesied.

Remember that grace is available to you. Last, remember your breakthrough has a name and it is called John, which as we said before means grace. Grace is available to you: *"And God is able to make all grace abound toward you..."* (2 Cor. 9:8).

Now that we have grace given to us, by and through Jesus, we can approach God's throne and receive that grace, mercy, and help in our times of need. Grace is an unmerited, undeserving favor that is a necessary ingredient to help us break through. This should be encouraging because it means we don't have to try to make it happen with our own power. We have a breaker spirit inside of us as Christians, and now we need to rise up and believe that we receive when we ask God and seek Him for breakthrough.

We can see in all these examples that grace always precedes breakthrough! We are no different than Zachariah and Elizabeth. We can apply these same principles and tap into the grace available to us. This is because inside every one of us who are born again through Jesus Christ, we possess the spirit and the ability to break through. We have been given the ingredients that we need. We just need to know how to bring them to birth, like any woman who is pregnant with a natural child.

Grace Meets Breakthrough

We possess the necessary ingredients inside of us to birth our breakthrough. We have been given grace and have it readily available to us in our pursuit of breakthrough and becoming a barrier breaker. It is so powerful when grace meets breakthrough. There is a synergy that happens when these two are working together to manifest breakthrough and blessings! We can see what happens when grace (John) meets Jesus the Breaker. It causes a response or a reaction, if you will. We find this when Elizabeth, who was six months pregnant with John, met Mary, who was pregnant with Jesus the Breaker! When these two met, something happened! The Bible says that the baby John (grace) leaped in the womb of his mother Elizabeth at the announcement and the meeting between her and Mary. Grace and Breakthrough were about to meet, and there would be a leaping or rejoicing as a response.

> *And it came to pass, that, when Elisabeth heard the salutation of Mary, the babe leaped in her womb; and Elisabeth was filled with the Holy Ghost...* *For, lo, as soon as the voice of thy salutation sounded in mine ears, the babe leaped in my womb for joy* (Luke 1:41,44).

It is the same way in the spirit when we position ourselves to tap into the grace that is made available to us, that it causes our breakthrough to come forth. It causes a response in the spirit like the leaping of John in the womb! When grace is a part of your breakthrough, God responds, angels respond, and you receive the answers to your prayers. Your breakthrough comes! Their meeting represents to us, spiritually speaking, the meeting of two elements of breakthrough. Grace needs a breakthrough while breakthrough needs grace to help prepare us to bring miracles forth. There is a key principle in the meeting of Elizabeth carrying John (grace) in her womb and Mary carrying Jesus (breakthrough) in her womb, which shows that grace and breakthrough must work together. Again, the reason John was born before the Breaker was that grace precedes breakthrough.

Another example of grace and breakthrough coming together that produces a heavenly response is also found when John baptized Jesus in the River Jordan. Once again, grace and breakthrough came together, which produced supernatural results. It is these same results that we can expect in our lives.

> *In those days Jesus came from Nazareth of Galilee and was baptized by John in the Jordan. And when He came up out of the water, at once he [John] saw the heavens torn open and the [Holy] Spirit like a dove coming down [to enter] into Him. And there came a voice out from within heaven, You are My Beloved Son; in You I am well pleased. Immediately the [Holy] Spirit [from within] drove Him out into the wilderness (desert)* (Mark 1:9-12 AMP).

Look at the powerful reaction of grace and breakthrough meeting. John baptizes Jesus and then the Bible records the following: the heavens were opened, which means access to God. Then it records the Holy Spirit entering in and becoming a part of your destiny. We also see God's voice speaking to give approval and direction! Finally, the Holy Spirit comes driving Jesus into the wilderness to be tempted of the devil. This means that there is grace available by the Holy Spirit, which moves you into victory over the devil.

Grace is available to us and helps us to become a barrier breaker. We also find this as we look at the clothing and the diet of John. The Bible says he wore camel hair and ate wild locusts and honey. Mark 1:6 (AMP) says, *"And John wore clothing woven of camel's hair and had a leather girdle around his loins and ate locusts and wild honey."* This doesn't sound like a wardrobe or a diet for most, now does it? However, from these natural examples we can apply spiritual, prophetic applications to how grace can help us if we will wear grace and keep it as a healthy source that we feed on spiritually. First, grace can help us to handle the burdens and the cares of this life. This prophetic truth is found in John's raiment of camel hair because a camel was a burden-bearing animal. It also reveals that grace is available to any burdens we may be facing. Now, wearing grace is not carrying our burdens around and letting them weigh us down, but it is giving them over to Jesus. This is why Jesus said, *"My yoke is easy, and My burdens is light"* (Matt. 11:30). This is because He walked in constant revelation of grace and as a result lived a life of breakthroughs.

Second, we see John eating locusts, which he was allowed to do under the law (see Lev. 11:22). This speaks to us prophetically about things that try to devour our lives and stop our harvest. Locusts are known for destroying crops, but the grace we have been given empowers our lives. It does it in a powerful way over the spiritual "locusts" sent to destroy our breakthrough. Instead of the locusts devouring us, we, like John, through grace devour them and eat them for lunch!

Third, the wild honey that John ate is what a life of grace and breakthrough gives us. Wild honey is what grace tastes like. It is so sweet when we step into full blessing and potential of what grace provides. So as barrier breakers, we can live in grace, handling the burdens of life, devouring our enemies, and living in an abundant life that is sweet and satisfying!

With John's name and his life, we have seen that it reveals an important principal ingredient of grace that is needed for breakthrough because it is connected to grace. In the Bible, names were very important in the Jewish tradition. In Jewish culture, your name has a significant meaning. You are what your name is. For example, Judah means "praise." Pharez means "breakthrough." Names spoke of character and revealed prophetic meaning.

When my wife, Brenda, and I had our two sons, Matthew and Jonathan, we prayed and asked God for names. We were asking the Lord to give us names in reference to something significant about their lives and destiny. Until the ultrasound we didn't know whether we were having boys or girls. So we asked the Lord to give us names. We were asking, expecting God to show us something prophetic and significant.

When our first son was born, the Lord told us He had given us His gift. We thought, "Wow! That is nice that God has given us His gift!" Yet, what we would soon find out was that He was speaking the meaning of what would become our son's name. We called him Matthew, which means the gift of God. He is certainly God's gift to us, and the older he gets the more of a gift he becomes. He is a strong, gifted leader and speaker who loves the Lord. He is truly the gift of God to us and to so many who have come to know him as well.

When my wife was pregnant with our younger son, we asked the Lord again, as we did with Matthew. We were sitting in the waiting room of the doctor's office when God spoke something to me. He said, "Jehovah has given." I then heard the name Jonathan. I remember leaning over to my wife, as we were ready to have the ultrasound in a few minutes, to tell her what I had heard. We both laughed and started to wonder if God was giving us a son. Sure enough! We named him Jonathan, which means "Jehovah has given."

I also remember, concerning Jonathan's birth, that the Lord told me the time he would be born. I mentioned to our doctor, with whom we had a friendly relationship, that the Lord told me the time our son would be born. He said, "OK, Hank, I will plan to be there at that time." Our son Jonathan was born at the exact time on the clock that the Lord said. It was a real sign from God. Jonathan, just as his name means, is truly a child the Lord has given to us, and he too is such a blessing, given to us by God. He has such a strong breakthrough spirit, an ability to pray, and a real love for the Lord. This shows how important names are.

If names aren't important, then have you ever considered why people don't often name their kids after criminals or people who are evil? For example, you don't find people calling their children jezebel, lucifer, satan, hitler, or nimrod. They usually will name them after someone or something good and will often choose biblical names like Noah, David, Paul, Luke, Mary, or Rachel, to name a few.

We see that names are especially true in the meaning of Judah's sons as they relate to those of us who need a breakthrough. We find a prophetic picture of how to birth our breakthrough moment and become a barrier breaker by studying the names of Judah's sons.

> *And the sons of Judah; Er, and Onan, and Shelah, and Pharez, and Zarah: but Er and Onan died in the land of Canaan. And the sons of Pharez were Hezron and Hamul* (Genesis 46:12).

In this verse, we see the progression and the ingredients to create a breakthrough. When you first read this verse in Scripture, it just looks like the mention of a few names of the sons of Judah, except these names in the Hebrew are a pattern to aid us in our breakthrough. It is not simply a bunch of purposeless names being listed. It is a prophetic progression that if you apply them, it will help birth your breakthrough moment.

Let's look at the meaning of their names and see how they are helpful ingredients.

- *Judah* = "praise"[1]
- *Er* = "watchful"[2]
- *Onan* = "strong"[3]
- *Shelah* = "prayer"[4]

- *Pharez* = "breakthrough"[5]
- *Zerah* = "sunrise" "sprout"[6]

Pharez's Sons:

- *Hezron* = "enclosure"[7]
- *Hamul* = "spared by God"[8]

As we look at the list of these names in the Hebrew and their meanings, we see the ingredients, progression, and the results of breakthrough if we apply them. We must start with praise (*Judah*). This opens the way in the spirit to bring our breakthrough forth, and it attracts God to our situations. As a result of our praise, we become watchful and discerning (*Er*) to anything that would try to steal our breakthrough. This enables us to remain sober, diligent, and watchful to carry our breakthrough seed to manifestation. This causes a spiritual strength (*Onan*) and endurance to keep our breakthrough spirit and not quit or give up until we have broken through. We do this by staying dedicated to prayer (*Shelah*). All of these ingredients—praise, *Judah*, watchful, *Er*, staying strong, *Onan*, and being dedicated to prayer, *Shelah*—then lead to our breakthrough, *Pharez*. It doesn't stop there, because the next thing, as we progress to birth our breakthrough moment, is that we receive the blessing. We then have the blessing of sunrise, sprouting (*Zerah*) that takes place. In other words, we have the new day and our breakthrough seed (Sunrise, *Zerah*) that started with a seed of praise (*Judah*) brings forth what we desire! Now the end result of breakthrough is also found in this list of Pharez's sons. After we have progressed as we mentioned, then we have breakthrough (*Pharez*) that comes, and it results in God's protection and covering (*Hezron*) and as a result we are spared by God (*Hamul*)!

We can see helpful ingredients from these examples with Judah's sons that lead to birthing our breakthrough moment. When all of these ingredients are put together, you have the results you desire!

It is important not to leave any out. The same is true in other areas of life. You can have all the ingredients you need, but if you don't follow directions or leave one of them out, it might not turn out correctly. An example of this would be in cooking. You can have all the ingredients set before you to make a cake, but if you leave one out and hurry through it, you can wind up with a disaster. I have done this several times when cooking, as I'm sure many of you have, and after doing all the hard work, waiting, and anticipating the eating enjoyment, it is frustrating when it doesn't taste right! There have been times when I had to completely start over because I skipped through directions or left out an important ingredient.

Putting all the necessary instructions and ingredients together is important to any barrier breaker. How many of us really like to read and follow the directions when it comes to building something? Too many times I have put things together only to discover when I am finished that they don't work, or are just not put together right because I didn't follow directions. Sometimes I have just skipped quickly through them trying to get to the final blessing of enjoying what I am building. I would rather look at the pictures and not read the directions thinking I can just build it and figure it out myself.

When my wife, Brenda, and I were having our first child, we began preparing the nursery. We were so excited to get started building things and putting together the baby crib and furniture, but we really didn't know what we were doing. I must admit Brenda has more skill with building things than I do. I often have to have her help me figure out why I didn't put something together right. We decided to assemble our newborn baby's crib. There we were, a happy, young, married couple working on our firstborn's baby crib. Everything seemed to be going along fine as I thought that I had followed the directions, but really I hadn't read them and had only just looked at the pictures. I hurried through the directions because I just wanted to see the final product!

Wow! We were finally done and it looked beautiful, except for one little problem. Why were there so many leftover parts? Everything seemed OK. After all, it's just a baby crib. The next thing we did was to put the baby mattress inside the newly built crib, when all of a sudden there was a noise and a shaking! Our beautiful masterpiece crib had just started to fall apart, with the mattress crashing down to the floor! Thank the Lord that there wasn't a baby in that crib! I humbly had to let Brenda figure out why it didn't work, and she successfully put it back together, safely!

Many times, like my examples of cooking or building a crib, we can be our own worst enemy in receiving or birthing our breakthrough moment. What do I mean by the enemy of our own breakthrough? One of the worst enemies is what I said before. It's wanting a handout rather than to birth a breakthrough for ourselves. Or maybe we are trying to force something rather than giving praise, staying strong, and being dedicated to prayer and stepping into the grace that we already have. Perhaps we are not being diligent to walk out the Word of God and continue to declare His promises. Maybe we feel like we have really made a mess of things and can't build or do anything right. I want you to be encouraged because you have grace! Remember, we can't, therefore God must! The key is that we don't have to abort our breakthrough. That is part of the devil's plan to get you frustrated and self-focused and eventually talking you into quitting, thus becoming an enemy of your own breakthrough moment.

If that's you, I want to encourage you that it is never too late to try to change. It always starts with little steps and small choices if you decide you want to change. The key is you are born to win and you are born to succeed. You just have to take a step and apply yourself to the principles of what we have read. You have grace in your time of need. We don't have to try to make it happen, nor do we need to sit back and do nothing. We don't have to be our worst enemy. We have grace to defeat the enemy and rise up and birth our breakthrough moment.

Enemies of your Breakthrough

When we establish what we need to do and are determined not to be the enemy of our own breakthrough, then we will seek our breakthrough.

If the devil can render you ineffective, then he can steal your breakthrough. The usual place he starts is with us, but if he can't use you to do it, then he will try some other ways. He tries to condemn you, accuse you, and make you think you can't do anything. The important thing is to realize the devil doesn't want you to break through and succeed. You must not be discouraged but realize there will always be things that try to stop, hinder, or abort your breakthrough.

That is just par for the course. This is what happened with Jesus. Herod, who was a wicked, perverted king, tried to stop the breakthrough as soon as he heard that Jesus was born. He set out to kill the baby, but he was unable to find Jesus, so he decided to have all babies two years of age and younger killed, hoping Jesus would be one of them (see Matt. 2:16).

The devil is always trying to use people to be pawns for his wicked plans. He did this when he used Herod and others to rise up against Jesus. He also did this with the apostle Paul by getting people to be demonically stirred up against him. This is why the Bible said he fought with the beasts at Ephesus. It wasn't that Paul was wrestling against natural beasts on his way to his meetings to preach. Instead, it meant he wrote to the church at Ephesus that his wrestling wasn't just against natural things but demonic spirits (see Eph. 6:12). The devil uses these spirits to come against humans to resist them and hinder them so they won't breakthrough. The beasts at Ephesus could also mean, as some have written in their commentaries, to imply that it was in reference to Paul reasoning with the Jews at Ephesus in Acts 18. Whatever the case, it is obvious that Paul had his run-in with many demonically-inspired people. Other commentaries say that the beasts of Ephesus were also implying Christians battling lions in a gladiatorial show. Whichever way we choose to believe, we can still, however, conclude that demons were the ultimate source of this behavior and attack against Paul and Christians no matter what the setting.

In one such example, we read an account when Paul was seeking a breakthrough from a buffeting spirit. This spirit was a thorn in Paul's flesh and was meant to hinder and stop his breakthrough.

> And lest I should be exalted above measure through the abundance of the revelations, there was given to me a thorn in the flesh, the messenger of Satan to buffet me, lest I should be exalted above measure. For this thing I besought the Lord thrice, that it might depart from me. And He said unto me, My grace is sufficient for thee: for My strength is made perfect in weakness (2 Corinthians 12:7-9).

So, this thorn in the flesh that Paul was speaking of wasn't all the things that religion and tradition has tried to speculate. It isn't difficult to see when the Bible tells us it was a messenger of Satan, a demon spirit, sent to stop his breakthrough. The devil goes about like a roaring lion seeking whom he may devour and seeking to kill, steal, and destroy your breakthrough. Did you notice the answer the Lord spoke to Paul that would help him in his breakthrough? The Lord told him it was grace that would be a key—the grace that he already possessed and just needed to lay a hold of by faith. It is this same grace that we saw before with John that is a key element to help us to break through any demonic resistance. Grace precedes breakthrough and is available to bring our victory!

We have victory over this devil and grace to withstand him given to us by Jesus. In fact, Psalm 91 lists three things we have victory and breakthrough over concerning things that the devil uses to stop our breakthrough.

> *Thou shalt tread upon the lion and adder: the young lion and the dragon shalt thou trample under feet* (Psalm 91:13).

Notice it says the lion, the adder, and the dragon, which are three prophetic things we have victory over.

1. *The lion*—these are the enemies of your breakthrough that look intimidating and come at you loudly and fearfully like a lion.

2. *The adder*—these are the small little things that come to nag you. Like the adder, which was a small snake not easy to detect, these little distractions and attacks are meant to steer you off course or hinder you in your breakthrough.

3. *The dragon*—these are the attacks that come against your mind or your thoughts. Just like a dragon doesn't exist, except in fantasy, these enemies of your breakthrough are things or circumstances the devil creates to make you think they exist but they really don't. This is so you will back off, and he uses them to hinder your breakthrough.

The devil uses these things to try to intimidate you and keep you from being a barrier breaker as well to hinder breakthrough. Sometimes these things can also be enemies of your breakthroughs that the devil often uses when you want to birth your breakthrough moment into manifestation. In the Books of Ezra and Nehemiah, we see examples of this as he used men called Sanballat and Tobiah to try to stop the building process of Nehemiah and the children of Israel. He sought to stop their breakthrough, and he still uses these same things to stop us from breaking through.

1. He tries to make you weak and weak handed.

    "Then the people of the land weakened the hands of the people of Judah" (Ezra 4:4).

2. He uses persecution, mocks you, and ridicules you.

    "But it came to pass, that when Sanballat heard that we builded the wall, he was wroth, and took great indignation, and mocked the Jews" (Nehemiah 4:1).

3. He tries to bring trouble to you.

    "And troubled them in building" (Ezra 4:4).

    "He uses people to give wrong advice and counsel. And hired counsellors against them, to frustrate their purpose ..." (Ezra 4:5).

4. He uses things to bring frustration.

    "To frustrate their purpose" (Ezra 4:5).

5. He stirs up accusations against you.

    "Wrote they unto him an accusation against the inhabitants of Judah and Jerusalem" (Ezra 4:6).

6. He causes people to conspire against you.

    "And conspired all of them together to come and to fight against Jerusalem, and to hinder it" (Nehemiah 4:8).

7. He spread lies and stirs up gossip about you.

"Then I sent unto him, saying, There are no such things done as thou sayest, but thou feignest them out of thine own heart" (Nehemiah 6:8).

8. He sends many distractions and uses people with wrong motives to hinder you.

Let us meet together in some one of the villages in the plain of Ono. But they thought to do me mischief" (Nehemiah 6:2).

9. He uses fear against you to stop you.

"For they all made us afraid, saying, Their hands shall be weakened from the work, that it be not done. Now therefore, O God, strengthen my hands" (Nehemiah 6:9).

Nehemiah and the children of Israel resisted these wicked schemes that the devil was trying to use to stop them and to hinder their breakthrough moment. If they prevailed, so can you. You have been given grace to bring your victory to pass, because the Greater One lives in you!

Your Scepter for Breakthrough

We have authority over the devil and his devices. We have been given the scepter of authority from Jesus the Breaker. The Bible says that even Judah had a scepter that would never leave him until the ultimate ruler comes. We know that ultimate ruler is the Lord.

> *The scepter shall not leave Judah; he'll keep a firm grip on the command staff until the ultimate ruler comes and the nations obey Him* (Genesis 49:10 MSG).

God had given the scepter to Judah that would be passed down to his descendants until it would lead to Jesus, the Breaker, and then to us! This scepter is now in the hands of Jesus and has also been given to us to rule and reign with Him. We can now use our authority we have been given. We can put our firm grip on it like with Jacob and the heel of his brother, or Judah with the scepter. We have a heavenly scepter and authority to be barrier breakers.

We have victory and grace available to us in Christ, the Breaker. The devil hates this thought and doesn't want you to have a breakthrough spirit like Pharez or to grip your scepter like Judah. The devil hates the grace and authority you have been given over him!

This is why when Jesus was being accused and they were ready to crucify him they put a reed in his hand to mock him.

> And when they had platted a crown of thorns, they put it upon His head, and a reed in His right hand: and they bowed the knee before Him, and mocked Him... (Matthew 27:29).

This was a mockery by the demon spirits, using man to insult Jesus and His Kingdom. These same spirits try to mock us and make it appear that we have no authority or power for breakthrough. How do we know this?

First, when they put a reed in Jesus' hand, this was to imply a scepter that was given to a king signifying ruler-ship or authority. This is why they mocked Him saying, "Hail, King of the Jews."

> ...and they bowed the knee before Him, and mocked Him, saying, Hail, King of the Jews! And they spit upon Him, and took the reed, and smote Him on the head (Matthew 27:29-30).

They were saying, "Look at you, Jesus, you have no authority, and your Kingdom has no power." We know that Jesus' Kingdom has power because even Pilate shot off his mouth acting like a big authoritative ruler up until Jesus spoke to him. He told Jesus, "Don't you know I have the power to crucify You?" I love Jesus' response here! He spoke back to Pilate and put things in perspective by saying, "You have no power unless it has been given to you by my Father. No man takes my life unless I lay it down."

> So Pilate said to Him, Will You not speak [even] to me? Do You not know that I have power (authority) to release You and I have power to crucify You? Jesus answered, You would not have any power or authority whatsoever

against (over) Me if it were not given you from above (John 19:9-11 AMP).

Wow, that's power! Immediately Pilate got a revelation of this King of kings and Lord of lords. The Bible says he washed his hands and had nothing more to do with this Jesus, releasing Him to the will of the people.

Second, we know that the demons, using men, mocked Jesus' Kingdom by using a reed. The reason they used a reed was to imply weakness because these large reeds, in the Middle East would blow in the direction the vehement desert wind was blowing and bend almost to the breaking point, but then snap back. They were comparing Jesus to a weak, powerless reed that bends in whatever direction the wind blows with no backbone. This is why Jesus said of John the Baptist, "What did you come out to see a reed shaking in the wind?" Matthew 11:7 says, *"And as they departed, Jesus began to say unto the multitudes concerning John, What went ye out into the wilderness to see? A reed shaken with the wind?"* By comparing John's ministry to a reed, He was saying that John was not wimpy and was not a "conform to the trends prophet" who just bent with popular opinion, but was a powerful prophet, unbending to men and submissive to God.

I say all this so you will know and realize just how powerful the grace and authority is that you have available as it has been given to us. Jesus gave us grace and authority to overcome. God, the Father, showed us this by giving Jesus a rod, a scepter, as the first thing He did when Jesus ascended! Notice what the Bible says God did.

> *But unto the Son He saith, Thy throne, O God, is for ever and ever: a sceptre of righteousness is the sceptre of Thy kingdom* (Hebrews 1:8).

Wow! God gave Jesus a scepter and called Him God, telling Him to sit down at His right hand. God was saying, "Take that, devil! My Son is not a wimpy Jesus, nor is His Kingdom or authority powerless. He is the Breaker, and I have given Him My scepter to prove it!" He lives in us! In fact, God didn't stop there! He gave that scepter for all who are in Christ. This scepter is no longer in the hands of the natural man, Judah, but it rests in the spiritual hands of the one called the Lion of the tribe of Judah!

And one of the elders saith unto me, Weep not: behold, the Lion of the tribe of Judah, the Root of David, hath prevailed to open the book, and to loose the seven seals thereof (Revelation 5:5).

This of course is speaking again of Jesus, the serpent crusher and Breaker! We are part of that heavenly tribe called the Church! Jesus said basically, "All power and authority has been given to Me, now go because I give you that same rod of authority, and remember I am with you always" (see Matt. 28:18-20). He was saying, "I, the Breaker, am in you to help you break through! You have My scepter of power, authority, and grace. Now go break through!"

Endnotes

1. Blue Letter Bible. "Dictionary and Word Search for *Yĕhuwdah (Strong's 3063)."* Blue Letter Bible. 1996-2010. 11 Aug 2010. < http://www. blueletterbible.org/lang/lexicon/Lexicon.cfm? strongs=H3063 >

2. Blue Letter Bible. "Dictionary and Word Search for *Er (Strong's 6147)."* Blue Letter Bible. 1996-2010. 11 Aug 2010. < http://www. blueletterbible.org/lang/lexicon/Lexicon.cfm? strongs=H6147 >

3. Blue Letter Bible. "Dictionary and Word Search for *Onan (Strong's 209)."* Blue Letter Bible. 1996-2010. 11 Aug 2010. < http://www. blueletterbible.org/lang/lexicon/Lexicon.cfm? strongs=H209>

4. Blue Letter Bible. "Dictionary and Word Search for *Shelah (Strong's 7956)."* Blue Letter Bible. 1996-2010. 11 Aug 2010. < http://www. blueletterbible.org/lang/lexicon/Lexicon.cfm? strongs=H7956>

5. Blue Letter Bible. "Dictionary and Word Search for *Pharez (Strong's 6555)."* Blue Letter Bible. 1996-2010. 11 Aug 2010. < http://www. blueletterbible.org/lang/lexicon/Lexicon.cfm? strongs=H6555>

6. Blue Letter Bible. "Dictionary and Word Search for *Zerah (Strong's 2226)."* Blue Letter Bible. 1996-2010. 11 Aug 2010. < http://www. blueletterbible.org/lang/lexicon/Lexicon.cfm? strongs=H2226>

7. Blue Letter Bible. "Dictionary and Word Search for *Hezron (Strong's 2696)."* Blue Letter Bible. 1996-2010. 11 Aug 2010. < http://www. blueletterbible.org/lang/lexicon/Lexicon.cfm? strongs=H2696>

8. Blue Letter Bible. "Dictionary and Word Search for *Hamul (Strong's*

2538)." Blue Letter Bible. 1996-2010. 11 Aug 2010. < http://www. blueletterbible.org/lang/lexicon/Lexicon.cfm? strongs=H2538>

John grew up and became
strong in spirit. And h
lived in the wilderness
until he began his public
ministry to Israe
(Luke 1:80 NLT)

Chapter Five

DEVELOPING A BARRIER-BREAKER SPIRIT

John grew up and became strong in spirit. And he lived in the wilderness until
he began his public ministry to Israel (Luke 1:80 NLT).

Hitting the concrete driveway, I swung the sledgehammer as hard as I
could, only to feel the vibrations of the cement go through my body,
but there were no signs of any breakthrough. Barely able to lift it, I swung the
hammer again. I was determined to crack the cement driveway that I was trying
to break apart. I had been hired to help a gentlemen break out an old cement
driveway to make room for a new one. I was barely a teenager at the time, and
the money seemed good, so I thought I would give it a try. I really couldn't get
out of it, however, because the man I was working for was a friend of my family
and my dad told him I would be there.

There I was on a very hot summer day, seeking a breakthrough on some
cement, but it would be to no avail. Does this sound like your situation? That
you are giving your best effort but not seeing even a small sign of any breakthrough? I was certainly overmatched and out of place in this new driveway
job. I kept trying to just get some little breaking of the concrete to appease my
own frustration. The hammer got heavier, and I got more tired. I was in no way
physically built for the kind of work that I had agreed to. After struggling for

quite a while, with no results, the man I was working for decided that I should work on something else. He suggested this, since he noticed I couldn't break the cement driveway. So, he began to swing the hammer like it was nothing and was breaking huge pieces of concrete like it was nothing! My job was now to pick up these pieces of cement and put them in the back of the truck. The only problem with that was I was a skinny little teenager, already tired from my sledgehammer moments. I was now barely able to lift the chunks of concrete.

I have always prided myself on hard work and felt a sense of honor to do my job the best I could. I started to try and lift the pieces in the truck, while my boss busily hammered away at the driveway. I put a few pieces in the truck, and then I went after the big one. I lifted a large piece of concrete barely up to the back of the truck, and just when I couldn't lift it any higher, the unthinkable happened! I fell backward, with the concrete piece landing on top of me. Thank the Lord my boss noticed and came over quickly and lifted the rock off of me and helped dust me off. Well, my first day was done, but it didn't take much to convince me, as I knew after those short hours of work, that I wasn't developed enough for this kind of desired breakthrough. It didn't take much to talk me into quitting and waiting until I was more developed and able to handle the kind of work.

The reason some of us don't experience breakthrough, like me with the concrete driveway, is not because we don't have the right equipment. I had the right equipment to get the job done, just like we have the grace and authority to get the job done in life. The reality is, we have the equipment and grace to break barriers, but we often haven't developed the strength and skill necessary to experience greater breakthroughs, so we keep swinging away at life with little to no results. This is where we have to grow and develop, just like John the Baptist and Jesus did. Remember, as discussed in the last chapter, they both prophetically represent to us grace and breakthrough.

Room for Breakthrough—Developing a Barrier-Breaker Spirit

There is nothing wrong with recognizing the need to grow and mature; even the Scriptures say John the Baptist and Jesus had to. I would rather see people recognize their immaturity in some areas so they can work on those things than have people who think they've got it together but don't.

It can often be awkward and uncomfortable as we grow and develop. A good example of this is going through puberty, because there are so many changes happening so quickly. This is why some don't want to grow spiritually either because it seems like it requires too much change and they are not used to it. Maturing and being willing to change is all a process of life. In our walk with God we are all at different levels and stages of our spiritual growth, as well. It is true that some people may lie down, others crawl, while others walk, and some may run; but ultimately as barrier breakers we are all called to soar. We may all be at different stages and experiencing different things, but we all need to identify them and be determined to grow from where we currently are. The important thing is that we rise up to our full potential in Christ and use the breaker spirit, grace, and authority that we have been given. Being a barrier breaker isn't based on our age. There is a vast difference between being young in the natural and young in the spirit. Just because someone may be young in the natural doesn't mean that they can't be old and mature in the spirit or vice versa. This was the way it was for Jesus and John the Baptist. They were young but mature and strong in the spirit (see Luke 1:80, 2:40,52). We even see Jesus speaking in the temple at the age of 12, astounding the people with His mature spirit and wisdom (see Luke 2:43, 46-47).

Jesus was demonstrating what we have mentioned throughout this book as what the Lord was and still is looking for. He is looking for that barrier-breaker spirit in humankind, no matter their age. As we said before, that power to break through already dwells in those who are Christians. We just need to grow and develop it into something greater and more powerful in our lives. We can see with John and Jesus that they too had to grow and develop into barrier breakers. The Bible says that they both grew up and became strong in the spirit.

- ### John the Baptist

   "And the child grew and became strong in spirit, and He was in the wilderness until the day of His public appearance to Israel" (Luke 1:80 ESV).

- **Jesus**

  "And the child grew and became strong, filled with wisdom. And the favor of God was upon Him" (Luke 2:40 ESV).

  "And Jesus increased in wisdom and in stature and in favor with God and man" (Luke 2:52 ESV).

These verses sound similar, even though they are written about two different people. It is because the Lord is telling us what He likes to see in a barrier breaker. As we look at these verses together, it reveals how to grow in grace (John) and receive our breakthroughs with Jesus.

Keep growing. The key is to make a decision to keep maturing and growing in your relationship with God, His Word, and a through a life of faith. There comes a time for all of us when we need to grow up spiritually and be weaned from the milk that belongs to young Christians. We need to become mature, strong believers feeding on the meat of God's Word (see Heb. 5:12-14). When we remember what John and Jesus' names mean and what their lives represent, then we better understand what they mean to us as barrier breakers. These references to John and Jesus growing are also prophetic references to us growing spiritually.

Become strong! Notice it says they "become" strong. This means it will require a choice, discipline, work, effort, and a process on our part to become strong barrier breakers. We can grow stronger in grace and our breakthrough in the spirit, but it doesn't come without working at it! That is what the Bible says about both John and Jesus; they grew strong in the spirit! The key to grace and breakthrough is a constant, daily life of growing and becoming stronger in our spiritual lives. We can't expect to become strong spiritually if we don't invest into our spiritual life. A healthy spiritual life consists of what I refer to as a four-legged table. All legs are essential for the table's stability. The four legs that are strength and stability to us are: 1) daily prayer, 2) daily Bible reading, 3) strong Christian relationships, and 4) being committed to a strong healthy church. John the Baptist and Jesus "became strong in spirit." It was in the spirit and not a reference to natural strength, even though they might have been naturally strong. This spiritual strength wasn't automatic, as we can see, because it says they became strong. It was a process to where they became strong in their spiritual lives and walk with God.

Grow in wisdom! Jesus "increased in wisdom." Again, it wasn't automatic just because He was the Son of God. He came as God in the flesh and had to study and apply human effort as well. He had to grow and attain godly and human wisdom. Wisdom is necessary for breakthrough and winning in spiritual battles (see Prov. 24:6). Too many times people want a breakthrough but don't use the wisdom and guidance of the Lord and then never reach their desired goals. It isn't a lack of grace or power available to you that keeps you from breakthrough but often a lack of appropriating godly wisdom.

Grow in the grace. This comes by walking in the grace you have been given by faith, pleasing God. The Bible says, *"But without faith it is impossible to please him"* (Heb. 11:6). We are saved by grace through faith, and we have been given this grace for breakthrough. We then need to continue to build our faith, walk in faith, and use our faith to bring breakthroughs into our lives through the grace given. The key is to seek to please God and grow in His grace.

We just need to be determined to rise up and take a hold of what is rightfully ours. That is what people of faith do. They don't have to settle for defeat, sickness, disease, premature death, accidents, injury, financial problems, or divorce, just to name a few! We don't have to be pushed around in life and feel that we are just staring at an unbreakable barrier, like the driveway I was trying to break. We possess the breaker spirit already in us, if we are in Christ. This isn't a matter of age, but it is a matter of recognizing and developing what we have already been given. We just need to keep developing as barrier breakers and rise to our fullest potential.

A good example of rising to our full potential so we can soar above our problems is found in the book of Job.

> *Is it by your understanding that the hawk soars, stretching his wings toward the south? Is it at your command that the eagle mounts up and makes his nest on high?* (Job 39:26-27 NASB)

Notice this verse says that the hawk flies and the eagle mounts up. These words to "fly" and "mount up" and the comparison of an eagle and hawk are symbolic of rising up in the spirit to overcome.

> *But they that wait upon the LORD shall renew their strength; they shall mount up with wings as eagles; they shall run, and not be weary; and they shall walk, and not faint* (Isaiah 40:31).

Barrier breakers wait on the Lord to receive strength and then mount up; they don't stay down! They flap their wings, soaring above life's challenges, and they won't faint or quit! We just have to decide to rise up in the grace that we have been given like the eagle! We can soar today; this is not tomorrow or some day in the future, but now is the time to rise up! The time to be determined to rise up and go to another level as a barrier breaker is right now!

I want to encourage you to not stop growing but strive to become stronger spiritually and keep growing in wisdom and the grace you have been given in Christ, because the things you need to develop in your life are closer than you think! They are in your own house. This is the way it was for Elisha the prophet. There was a Shunemite woman and her husband who made a room to accommodate this prophet. In this room were several provisions to help accommodate his breakthrough ministry. Elisha was developing into more of a barrier breaker. The Shunemite woman was also about to get a major breakthrough from Elisha's ministry. The items she provided for him in his room prophetically represent the resources we need for creating our own breakthroughs.

> *Let us make a little chamber, I pray thee, on the wall; and let us set for him there a bed, and a table, and a stool, and a candlestick: and it shall be, when he cometh to us, that he shall turn in thither* (2 Kings 4:10).

- *Chamber*—This is your prayer closet to meet with God (see Matt. 6:6)
- *Bed*—The place where you hear from God and talk to Him (see Ps. 63:6)

- *Table*—Used to study the Word of God and feed on it (see 2 Tim. 2:15)

- *Stool*—The place you learn your authority in Christ (see Eph. 2:6)

- *Candlestick*—This is used to see, or get revelation (see Eph. 1:17)

It was all of these things, in the natural, in Elisha's room that helped further develop him spiritually into a barrier breaker. It was also these resources that helped bring breakthrough when it was needed most. We have these same tools available to produce breakthroughs in our lives as well. If we apply them, they will prepare us for the times we may need to break through.

This Shunemite woman would experience two major breakthroughs as a result. She received one of them when she couldn't conceive and the prophet prophesied that she would.

> *"About this time next year," Elisha said, "you will hold a son in your arms."*
> *"No, my lord," she objected. "Don't mislead your servant, O man of God!"*
> *But the woman became pregnant, and the next year about that same time she*
> *gave birth to a son, just as Elisha had told her* (2 Kings 4:16-17 NIV).

How did this woman create her breakthrough? It started by a seed of hospitality she and her husband started when they gave Elisha a room in which to stay. This started the process of their breakthrough that later produced breakthroughs in their lives when they would need it. The woman and her husband received a second breakthrough when the child she had (even though she had previously been barren) later died and was brought back to life (see 2 Kings 4:18-36). She exhibited a breaker spirit after the death of her son, prophesied by Elisha, as she never quit and refused to speak wrong or get into doubt and unbelief.

> *So she went and came unto the man of God to mount Carmel. And it came*
> *to pass, when the man of God saw her afar off, that he said to Gehazi his*
> *servant, Behold, yonder is that Shunammite: Run now, I pray thee, to meet*

her, and say unto her, Is it well with thee? is it well with thy husband? is it well with the child? And she answered, It is well (2 Kings 4:25-26).

In the midst of a tragedy, she remained faithful to believe and work toward her breakthrough without giving up. She was so determined her son would rise again that she wouldn't say anything to the contrary. The child was then miraculously brought back to life through Elisha. Why? I believe it was the initial generosity of the woman and her husband to provide a room for Elisha that was a seed that helped to birth her breakthrough. I also believe it was her breaker spirit and the things Elisha had in his room that all culminated in her receiving breakthrough. We have these same things available today that will help us in becoming a greater barrier breaker!

Break Through the Ceiling—Send Judah First

The opportunity for breakthrough may be right in our room and some-times we don't recognize it. This happened in Jesus' ministry when the Bible said the power of the Lord was present to heal all in the room, except no one in the room tapped into the power to break through, until one man sick of the palsy received his healing because some men lowered him on a stretcher through the roof. There was no room to get in where Jesus was ministering, so they broke through the roof. They literally tore the roof off! They were so determined with a breakthrough mentality to get to the power available in that room that they ripped through the ceiling.

This is the same kind of breakthrough spirit we need if we want to experience victory and see our needs met. We have to be willing to break through whatever ceiling or barrier is in the way of our breakthrough! The reason they got a breakthrough was because they discerned the power and the potential for breakthrough in the room. Just like with Elisha and his room, there were ample resources available to create a breakthrough. Jesus the Breaker and His power were present in that room for all who would lay hold of it. Their determination to break through a barrier with faith helped them to create their breakthrough moment (see Luke 5:17-20)!

My wife, Brenda Kunneman, mentions a powerful thing in her book enti-tled *When Your Life Has Been Tampered With* that reveals why many don't experience a life of breakthrough. In Chapter 2 she wrote "Many Christians have the tendency, to 'wish for,' rather than 'create,' their breakthrough." [1] We can't just wish for breakthrough; we need to create it with faith.

Those men could have just *wished* they were inside the room where the breakthrough was available, but instead they reached down on the inside of themselves. They tapped into faith in God that if they could break through the roof they could receive their breakthrough for the man on the stretcher. One of the greatest ways to create a breakthrough in our lives is by praising God. Some of the most powerful barrier breakers are those who praise God. It is praise, worship, and intimacy with God that are vital for a continued life of victory and answered prayer. I am convinced if people realized this they would praise God more and experience more breakthroughs in their lives.

What makes praise so powerful is that it is a weapon against the enemy and brings deliverance from bondage. When Paul and Silas were thrown in jail for preaching the gospel, they did something that led to their breakthrough. While they were in jail and in chains, they praised and magnified God! They broke through the ceiling of bondage of being in prison, and as a result their chains fell and they were free (see Acts 16:25-26).

Paul and Silas didn't give up or wait until they experienced a breakthrough to praise and thank God. They created their breakthrough in the midst of difficult circumstances by praising God. They broke through the ceiling of demonic resistance that led to their freedom. When they praised God, they received the breakthrough they desired, and so can you! When you feel bound and as though you are in darkness and then praise your way to breakthrough!

The other powerful thing about praise is it attracts God to your situation, especially when you declare His name according to your situation. The Bible says that when we praise, God comes and inhabits our praise (see Ps. 22:3). Our praise brings God on the scene, and He goes before us to break through for us and leads us into victory.

We find this was true when King Jehoshaphat was in need of a break-through for himself and the people. His answer was not in the natural armies of his kingdom alone but the praise of the people. The way Jehoshaphat received his breakthrough was by sending praise (Judah) first. There was a great victory for him and his kingdom because of praise. The Scripture says:

> ...He appointed singers unto the LORD, and that should praise the beauty of holiness, as they went out before the army, and to say, Praise the LORD; for His mercy endureth for ever. And when they began to sing and to praise, the LORD set ambushments against the children of Ammon, Moab, and mount Seir, which were come against Judah; and they were smitten. (2 Chronicles 20:21-22).

We can see from Judah how we can receive a breakthrough. As we mentioned before, the name Judah in the Hebrew means praise. There is power in our praise that gets God's attention and can also defeat the enemy. Praise helps to lift the ceiling of oppression and resistance that often tries to prevent our breakthroughs! Our praise is a weapon that breaks through the enemy opposition and brings the Lord on the scene to defeat the devil. It was the sending of Judah in praise that was the key. This wouldn't be the first time that the tribe of Judah was sent ahead. Many times in Scripture the tribe of Judah was sent first into battle (see Josh. 1:1-2). The reason for this was that it signified the power of our praise to win in the battles of life by sending Judah first. Why was Judah sent first? One reason is because his father, Jacob, prophesied and declared this blessing on his son, Judah, by saying that even his brothers would praise him. He also prophesied that Judah (praise) would triumph over all of his enemies with a scepter. Another reason Judah was sent first was for us to see that we can use praise to break open the way to have victory over the enemy. The word "Judah" also means to hold out your hand and throw or shoot either a stone or an arrow at your enemy. This helps us to see how powerful praise is against the enemy and how powerful it is for breakthrough.

As we develop in our lives, like Jesus and John the Baptist did, we too will wax strong in the spirit. The more we make praise a part of our lives and develop it, the more we will see the benefits of it. I want you to see what praising God first and how incorporating it in you life will have great rewards. The names and the meanings of Judah's descendents reveal the benefits of praise and how it leads to blessings. *"The descendants of Judah were Perez, Hezron, Carmi, Hur, and Shobal"* (1 Chron. 4:1 NLT).

Judah = Praise[2]

Pharez = Breakthrough[3]

Hezron = Covering, Protection[4]

Carmi = Gardner of a vineyard[5]

Hur = White[6]

Shobal = A place of overflowing[7]

From this Scripture in Chronicles, we see how to develop a barrier-breaking spirit in our life, and it starts with praise. We start with (Judah) praise and worshiping God in all we do. This leads to and helps produce a breakthrough (Pharez). As a result of our praise and a breakthrough, we then are covered and protected by God's presence (Hezron). This progression is so powerful that as a result, we begin to see the things that we believe for come to fruition and harvest (Carmi). A continued life of purity (Hur) will help, as we praise, to experience God's presence and breakthrough blessings. When we continue to make this our way of life, we then enter into a place of continual overflow of blessings and breakthrough (Shobal)!

When would be a good time to praise God? How about like Hannah when she praised God, which birthed her breakthrough moment. The Bible tells us some things about her situation that were barriers to her breakthrough (see 1 Sam. 1:1-28).

She had no children (see verse 2). No fruit or desires of her heart had been met.

Her womb was shut (see verse 5). She had no answer to her prayer.

Her adversary provoked her sore (see verse 6). She was under satanic attack through another person.

She was accused falsely (see verse 14). She was misunderstood and accused of being drunk.

Yet, she praised God anyway and received her breakthrough. In spite of all these negative barriers she continued, year after year, worshiping and offering sacrifices unto God (see 1 Samuel 1: 3). She stayed faithful even when she kept being attacked by her adversary. She eventually broke through!

Maybe you feel like Hannah, just hoping the frustrations and the onslaught of hell would stop against you. It doesn't come by hoping but by action, like Hannah, who kept praying.

Have you ever heard a noisy door swing on a hinge? I once had a gate on my fence that was so noisy and every time it was opened, or the wind blew, it would make a horrible screeching sound. Do you know what the solution to this problem was? I went in and got some oil and greased the hinges. It had to come in contact with the oil by my choice or action. It wasn't in hoping or complaining about it that brought me peace from that fence, but it was in my action. This is the same solution for us today. When you praise God and resist the devil, instead of just hoping it will get better, the power of God is released. The devil backs off and quiets down. With the release of God's power and His anointing in your situation, as the Scripture says concerning the anointing oil, you will break yokes and undo heavy burdens (see Isa. 10:27).

This is also what David did to help King Saul get a breakthrough. It required action and his praise to release the presence of God and the anointing of the Holy Spirit. It was not a breakthrough for himself, but for someone else. He helped King Saul get relief from the evil spirit attacking him.

> *And Jesse took an ass laden with bread, and a bottle of wine, and a kid, and sent them by David his son unto Saul.... And it came to pass, when the evil spirit from God was upon Saul, that David took an harp, and played with his hand: so Saul was refreshed, and was well, and the evil spirit departed from him* (1 Samuel 16:20,23).

How did David help King Saul get a breakthrough? It started with praise just like we saw with the names of Judah's sons. David helped Saul, showing us how we too can get a breakthrough when we are under attack. He helped to lift a ceiling of torment and heaviness in Saul's life. From these verses, we can see the things David provided for Saul's breakthrough.

- Get around *"breakthrough believers"* (Saul called on David to help break through).
- We need *"bread"* (Stay in the word of God).
- Carry the *"new wine"* in you (Stay full of the Holy Spirit and pray tongues!)
- Acts 2—New wine!
- Don't forget the *"kid" (goat)!* (Sacrifice and worship help us to break through.)
- Bring the *"harp"* (David praised God, causing the devil to leave.)

David was a powerful barrier breaker who understood the power of praise. Some of the most breakthrough type songs are in the book of Psalms and were written by David. He developed into a barrier breaker from the time he was young and became even stronger by the time he was king. Again, David was a descendent of Judah and Pharez.

> *The family tree of Jesus Christ, David's son, Abraham's son: Abraham had Isaac, Isaac had Jacob, Jacob had Judah and his brothers, Judah had Perez and Zerah (the mother was Tamar), Perez had Hezron, Hezron had Aram, Aram had Amminadab, Amminadab had Nahshon, Nahshon had Salmon, Salmon had Boaz (his mother was Rahab), Boaz had Obed (Ruth was the mother), Obed had Jesse, Jesse had David, and David became king* (Matthew 1:1-6 MSG).

You could say that David had this barrier-breaker spirit in his family genes, because all these people had the same spirit. He used his slingshot to kill a lion and a bear, and then Goliath. The Bible gives us a description of this mighty barrier breaker that we can apply to our lives and continue to develop. The important thing to understand is that David grew into a barrier breaker, and it developed in him over time.

Then one of the young men said, "Behold, I have seen a son of Jesse the Bethlehemite who is a skillful musician, a mighty man of valor, a warrior, one prudent in speech, and a handsome man; and the LORD is with him" (I Samuel 16:18 NASB).

This verse is another example showing the characteristics of David as a barrier breaker. He was a young man developing into a warrior and a skillful musician. He kept developing in his skill and in his praise to God, becoming a mighty man of valor and even a risk taker. The time that he spent praising God caused him to have wisdom. The result was that he became prudent in speech and wise with his words. This verse also referred to David as being handsome, which means he probably took care of himself. The best part was that he walked with God, and the hand of the Lord was with him. This caused him to enjoy the Lord's blessing on his life. However, the root of David's success was in his heart and praise to God.

All of these things that describe David are rooted in his pursuing and developing into a man after God's own heart. He showed this by his continual desire and love for God. It's what made David different than King Saul, who needed David to praise God for him. True barrier breakers are like David in that they can praise God on their own. They aren't dependent on the right setting, mood, worship song, or music to help them praise. Sauls are different in that they have somewhat of a Zerah spirit, a handout mentality. They need others to constantly help pray and praise God for them so they can experience breakthrough, relief from the enemy, or intimacy with God. Saul was tired and tormented and didn't know how to break through for himself. There is nothing wrong with helping others like David did, or requesting help; it just shouldn't be our habit or way of life. We have to learn how to create breakthrough for ourselves and tear through the ceilings of resistance.

Put Your Foot Down!

At some point you have to put your foot down and say enough is enough! Shake off the attacks of the devil and the things trying to bind you by praising

God. This is like sending Judah (praise) first. You may be saying you are too tired to praise! Well you need to shake it off! Remember, it was praise that refreshed King Saul's life and will refresh yours also. It was praise that broke through the ceiling of torment and oppression. Years ago we used to sing a song in church that said, "Lift up your holy hands and shake off those heavy bands." This is why praise, as we mentioned, is so powerful when it comes to becoming a barrier breaker, because as you lift up holy hands to God, you begin to shake off the heavy bands!

This is what the apostle Paul did when he was attacked. A snake bit him on the Island of Malta.

> *Once we were safe on shore, we learned that we were on the island of Malta. The people of the island were very kind to us. It was cold and rainy, so they built a fire on the shore to welcome us. As Paul gathered an armful of sticks and was laying them on the fire, a poisonous snake, driven out by the heat, bit him on the hand. The people of the island saw it hanging from his hand and said to each other, "A murderer, no doubt! Though he escaped the sea, justice will not permit him to live." But Paul shook off the snake into the fire and was unharmed. The people waited for him to swell up or suddenly drop dead. But when they had waited a long time and saw that he wasn't harmed, they changed their minds and decided he was a god* (Acts 28:1-6 NLT).

He didn't freak out like I did with the snakes! He didn't glorify the devil, draw attention, or quit and just lie down. Had he laid down, he probably would have died. Yet, there was something inside of Paul that caused him to overcome. You guessed it! He had that barrier-breaker spirit that we read about in Scripture. There was nobody who could help him with his need for breakthrough that day. He was going to have to draw from the revelation of who he was in Christ and what he had been given in order to overcome.

He was ready for victory because he said he prayed in tongues more than many in the church at the time (see 1 Cor. 14:18). Praying in tongues helped prepare him and gave him a strong spirit (see Jude 20). He also developed a life of praise and trust in God by praising God in prison (see Acts 16). All of those times of prayer, praise, and building up his spirit helped to create and develop him into a barrier breaker.

Do you realize all that came against him? All the shipwrecks, the spirit that came to buffet him, a thorn in the flesh, persecutions, beatings, and now this serpent? Paul overcame! Why? Because he tapped into the grace given to him that God said was sufficient for him when he had a thorn in his flesh. He did what we have been talking about: he foreran his breakthroughs with grace by all the times he spent developing his spiritual walk. How did he develop into grace? He prayed in the spirit, and he knew God's Word and studied it. He praised, sending Judah first into his battles. As a result, the Bible said he overcame. He broke through, and so can you. Shake it off and loose yourself from captivity just like Paul shook off the poisonous snake. You can do this by drawing a line in the sand and putting your foot down.

This requires you to literally shake off your troubles and start praising God! You can shake off and put your foot down on whatever is attacking you. You can have victory just like apostle Paul did and put your foot down as a barrier breaker! What do I mean by putting your foot down? By rising up as a barrier breaker and using the grace, the scepter of authority you have been given, in order to stop something from happening. This scepter of authority has never left Judah because it was passed down to Jesus and given to us. Now we can exercise our scepter of authority every time we praise God. We can put our foot down by praising and being decisive and making a choice to say enough is enough!

Jesus put His foot down on the devil. The devil thought he had won when he crucified Jesus. He thought he had Jesus in his grip. Yet, when they pierced Jesus' body, especially His feet, the prophetic mystery of Genesis 3:15 was unfolding. The serpent crusher, Jesus, was crushing the devil and bringing breakthrough for you and me. All the devil was doing, by piercing Jesus' feet, was bruising his heel!

When Jesus had his feet pierced as he was crucified, it marked the bruising of his heel by the enemy, but something greater was happening. He was fulfilling Genesis 3:15 that he would crush the devil's head. What do we mean by crushing the devil's head? He was crushing satan's headship, authority, kingdoms, influence, and power. Jesus put his foot down, and all things are now under His feet (see Ps. 8:6). The powerful thing is we are now the Lord's spiritual feet in His body called the Church. We, as the seed of Christ, corporately fulfill this prophecy in Genesis 3 as the Body of Christ. We, as barrier breakers, have been given the authority in Him to put our feet down and exercise the grace, power, and authority for breakthrough. As barrier breakers, we have the authority to put our feet down upon the devil and demand our breakthroughs. You are the feet now that will continue to do the crushing to the enemies of darkness. You can trample their plans against you and stop their maneuvers that try to keep your breakthrough from happening. The Bible is full of examples of feet related to authority, dominion, and breakthrough:

- Every place the sole of your feet shall tread you have victory—Joshua 1:3

- You can "tread' upon all the power of the devil—Luke 10:19

- You will trample the lion, adder, and dragon under your "foot"—Psalm 91

- Has crushed satan beneath your feet—Romans 16:20

Now you need to put your foot down and decide you are no longer going to keep letting the devil push you around. That is what a barrier breaker does.

Feet were an important part of the Jewish culture. Jesus illustrated this when He was demonstrating servanthood and humility by washing His disciples' feet. There are references in the Bible to feet that speak of authority, your path or direction, or bowing down and worshiping at the Lord's feet. It can also represent our walk and conduct. Another example would be when David showed his authority and dominion over Goliath. The Bible says that after he killed him, David put his feet on his neck and cut off his head. This was speaking of victory and that David had broken through and this enemy wouldn't rise again.

God also told Joshua that every place his feet would tread, God had given him a breakthrough of dominion (see Josh. 1:3). I challenge you, just as God told Joshua, to put your foot down! You need to put your foot down in God's promises and say, "I'm not going to give in to defeat..." This is the heart of a barrier breaker!

The problem with many today is they don't use, or fully understand, the authority they have in Christ to put their feet down. They often let the devil push them around rather than putting their foot on him and resisting him and stopping him. We should always remember: "Big God, little devil!" Always be careful not to magnify your problems or the devil over the greatness of God. This gives the devil more power. An example of this would be with Paul, who was called Saul at the time. He was persecuting the Church and thinking he was doing it justly. The picture I want you to see is the literal meaning of what Jesus said to him when he was confronted on the way to Damascus. Here Paul relates what Jesus said to him in Hebrew.

> And when we were all fallen to the earth, I heard a voice speaking unto me, and saying in the Hebrew tongue, Saul, Saul, why persecutest thou Me? It is hard for thee to kick against the pricks (Acts 26:14).

You can't expect to pick a fight with God and think you are going to win. The definition in the Greek for "kicking against the pricks" is active resistance against a stronger power. In other words, Saul (Paul), the lesser power, was challenging and resisting a greater power. Of course, it was Jesus who Paul was attempting to overpower.

This is exactly what the devil does to stop our breakthrough. As the weaker power, He pushes against us and against God. He is not equal in power to God or the power we have been given, but because many refuse to put their foot down on him, he continues to push against us. The sad thing is that he does it even though he has been stripped of his power and authority! In the case with Saul (Paul), he was the weaker vessel who was persecuting Christians, but ultimately it was the greater power of God that he was pressing against.

We have the same authority to put the devil under our feet. He is the lesser power pressing against the greater power like Saul was with Jesus.

You are more sure-footed and anointed for breakthrough than you realize. We have been given hinds' feet.

> *The Lord God is my Strength, my personal bravery, and my invincible army; He makes my feet like hinds' feet and will make me to walk [not to stand still in terror, but to walk] and make [spiritual] progress upon my high places [of trouble, suffering, or responsibility]!* (Habakkuk 3:19 AMP).

This speaks of strength and being spiritually sure-footed. We are not easily moved from our position and have feet that can live on top and not on the bottom of life!

Years ago, before I was in full-time ministry, I had to put my foot down and not be moved from my position of standing for righteousness on my job at the time. I was required by my employer to attend a weekend training seminar out of town. Everyone at my job knew that I was very dedicated to my Christian faith, but they would still purposely make comments in opposition to me. I was instructed by my boss that I was going to have to go on the trip with a couple other guys to a city several hours away. Of course, they didn't like me coming and purposely played the music loud in the company car while I listened to my Christian music in my headphones.

After several hours, they started to look for a place to stop and eat lunch. I suggested the city where my father-in-law lived since it was right off the interstate and it wasn't too much farther down the road we were on. I suggested it because I could possibly meet my father-in-law for lunch. These fellow employees and travel companions would have nothing of the sort, especially once they knew that I wanted to see my dad. They kept driving, on purpose, just to try to make me mad. So, we had lunch somewhere else and finally reached the hotel where the seminar was being held.

We arrived at the hotel and had the evening to ourselves before the seminar started the next day. We had joining rooms with roommates to cut down on the costs. I stayed in my room while my co-workers went down for happy hour. I was talking to my wife on the phone when my boss and some of the other guys came into the room. They informed me I had to hang up the phone because they needed a driver that night. I hung up the phone, only to discover they wanted me to be the designated driver so they could go to a strip club and get drunk. Politely, I told my boss that I wasn't going to be the driver, nor would I go with them. I told them that it was not right for me as a Christian to go to a strip club. He then began to mock me, suggesting I just wait out in the company car while they were inside the club.

That's when I put my foot down! I didn't care what the repercussions would be, I wasn't going to compromise! He left angrily, threatening that I would be called into his office to deal with my behavior when the seminar was over. And guess what, he did. He fired me for insubordination when we got back from the seminar. What was so insubordinate about standing up for moral and Christian conduct?

I must tell you, though, while they were gone to the club that night, I prayed over their rooms and beds. Later on that night they complained they couldn't sleep! So they slept on the floor or in a chair, restless the entire night. They kept asking me what I did to the room.

They all found my presence a burden, so the boss made me leave early and ordered the same two guys I rode there with to drive me home. On the way home, they were even madder at me because the boss made them take me back early. They already had little sleep because of their previous night of escapades, and now they had to drive me home! I invaded their life by putting my foot down for righteousness.

Do you know what happened? Remember how I had suggested stopping in the city where my father-in-law lived for lunch but they had refused? This time I prayed because I really wanted to stop in and see him. God as my witness, after praying, we began to experience car problems. The car was losing power and acting strangely. We finally had no option but to exit the interstate right at the exit where my mother-in-law worked! So, I walked over to see her and arranged lunch with my father-in-law on his birthday. I tell you, God is so funny! While those guys waited for the tow truck on the side of the road for several hours, my father-in-law picked me up, and I went to lunch. After my lunch was over, the mechanic told my co-workers he couldn't find anything wrong with the car. While they waited for the car to be looked at, I was off celebrating my father-in-law's birthday all afternoon. God blessed me greatly because I put my foot down in righteousness, and God defended me and gave me a breakthrough!

If the enemy has put his foot in your situation, then you need to put your foot down and draw a line in the sand.

Drawing a Line in the Sand

Drawing a line in the sand is based on the idea of literally making a mark in sand to show someone they cannot move across it. If you draw a line in the sand, then you establish a limit for which certain things that cross that line are considered unacceptable.

An example of this reminds me of a time when I was being bullied at school by someone who was a lot bigger than me. I was in elementary school and was tired of being pushed around by this big, oversized kid, in my opinion. It was field day, a day where students compete in various track events, and I had signed up for the running long jump. This is where you run as fast as you can and then at the designated line you jump as far as you can. The place you jump into is filled with sand so you have a soft landing. Wherever you land in the sand is the measurement of your jump.

Well, I finally decided I had had enough of this bully, who had been push-ing me around all day at the track event, so I finally drew a line in the sand. I took my foot in the long jump sand pit and drew a line. I told him that enough was enough, and I wasn't going to take it anymore. I was drawing a line in the sand indicating that I was rising up a resistance and determination to do some-thing. The only problem with my line in the sand was as soon as I drew it, he said, "Oh, yeah?" and stepped over the line and started punching me! I was too intimidated at the time to fight back, and the teacher broke it up.

The bullying continued for years after because the bully knew I didn't believe I could beat him. But there comes a day when you decide you won't tolerate the bully anymore. I eventually drew another line in the sand, so to speak, with this same guy a few years later. I had enough and fought back so hard and fast he didn't know what hit him. He never messed with me after that because I drew a line in the sand for real that time. With everything in me, I had decided I wasn't taking it anymore.

To draw a line in the sand is also saying, "What are you standing for?" God drew a line in the sand to see which side the people would stand on. He wanted to see if they were on His side or the devil's (see Num. 16).

Joshua also drew a line in the sand. Toward the end of Joshua's life, he made this statement, as recorded in Joshua 24:15 (NASB), *"Choose for yourselves today whom you will serve: ...but as for me and my house, we will serve the Lord."*

Joshua was telling the people of Israel to draw a line in the sand, so to speak. He was telling them to choose one side of the line and make their stand. To stand on the side of their forefathers would cause them defeat and ultimate destruction, but to stand on the side of the Lord would bring them blessing and success (see Josh. 1:8-9).

Ask yourself, on which side of the line do you stand concerning your situation? Are you standing on the Lord's side of righteousness and trusting in Him? Or are you standing on the side of rebellion or fear and defeat? Are you putting up with the devil and his bullying, or are you going to step into the grace and authority you have been given to stop him?

The family line of Abraham, Isaac, and Jacob that led to Christ was a spiritual bloodline drawn to let the devil know where God stands. God always wanted a people who would stand with Him. Throughout history, God was trying to get people to draw a line in the sand by trying to get them to cross over; examples are with the Red Sea and the River Jordan. These were both natural lines that needed to be crossed and designed to mark a point where the people would never go back. If they would cross the river and sea, then it would lead them further away from previous bondage into their breakthrough and inheritance. The only problem was they complained on the way, even after God drew a line in the sand at the Red Sea by opening up the sea and swallowing Pharaoh and his army. God was showing Israel whose side He was on. Yet,

Israel wouldn't draw that line with God and often wanted to go back to the bondage they came out of (see Num. 14:3).

There are many reasons why people don't want to cross the line, like Israel, or draw the line. They often give excuses as to why they can't do it or they think the path is too difficult and impossible, like with the crossing of the Red Sea. Another reason people won't cross the line, like with Israel, is because they become too comfortable with their surroundings and lifestyle. They like the way things used to be and do want to enter unfamiliar territory. So they develop a mind-set of never breaking through but rather settling for their current situation or whatever life gives them just because it is familiar. Some won't cross the line because of fear. It can be fear of the unknown, fear of change, or fear of the enemy. Fear renders many ineffective, as it keeps them in neutral or causes them to go in reverse rather than forward and crossing the line into their promised victory.

It wasn't until a whole generation passed that the children of Israel finally crossed the line into their inheritance. It was only Joshua and Caleb, of the prior generation, who crossed the line. It was because they had already crossed the line before as spies and came back with the determination for Israel to break through. The Bible says they had a different spirit (see Num. 14:24 NIV). They had a different spirit in that it was a barrier-breaker spirit. It is the same kind of spirit we have and are to enforce now that we have Jesus Christ in our lives.

As you develop into a barrier breaker, settle it in your heart that you want to be one who develops into a powerful barrier breaker. In order to do this, just start off small and progress. It's small steps, line after line. When you are developing your barrier-breaker mind-set, spirit, and lifestyle, it's important to be consistent and open to change. It is too often that we keep on the same course with the same old mind-sets, habits, and routines and never change. This is what God said to the children of Israel, He told them to change their direction and get going!

> *Then we turned, and took our journey into the wilderness by the way of*
> *the Red sea, as the LORD spake unto me: and we compassed Mount Seir*

many days. And the LORD spake unto me, saying, Ye have compassed this mountain long enough: turn you northward (Deuteronomy 2:1-3).

Remember, there is power in the right agreement. Find someone who can encourage you and help, like when Mary met Elizabeth, who was pregnant with John. The Bible says her baby leaped (see Luke 1). In other words, get around people who cause what is inside you to come alive and break through. Being around the same ol' depressed, gossiping, compromising, inconsistent, and lazy folks who have "chicken" spirits isn't going to turn you into a barrier breaker or make your breakthrough leap! One of the biggest problems some people have in becoming and developing into a barrier breaker is the older they get the more set in their ways they become. This is true both naturally and spiritually. It is important not to become resistant and stubborn to growth, effort, and change, especially when it doesn't look like any breakthrough is happening.

Keeping your attitudes in check will go a long way in your success in life and what you want in answered prayer or in your victories. If you don't keep your attitudes right you can get into complaining and go backward instead of forward into breakthrough. This is what happened to the children of Israel. They complained, and God heard and became angry. The children of Israel's complaining made some want to go back to Egypt! What was in Egypt? Bondage and an oppressor! Does that sound like breakthrough? No! There isn't anything exciting about being in bondage! A great way to become a barrier breaker is to avoid complaining and just start celebrating small changes and blessings. This is especially true when it doesn't look like breakthrough is eminent. Keep praising and pressing through. It's small steps and small changes. Remember, in all things give thanks unto God and rejoice evermore (see 1 Thess. 5:16)!

Celebrate small changes, even if they don't seem like much. You can grow and develop into a barrier breaker, wax strong in spirit, and live a life of praise that breaks through! The Breaker is in you; rise up! Put your foot down and draw a line in the sand. It's time for your continual breakthrough moment as you praise God, sending Judah before you into battle!

Endnotes

1. Brenda Kunneman, *When Your Life Has Been Tampered With* (Charisma House, 2008), Chapter 2, p. 29.

2. Blue Letter Bible. "Dictionary and Word Search for *Judah (Strong's 3063)*." Blue Letter Bible. 1996-2010. 11 Aug 2010. < http://www.blueletterbible.org/lang/lexicon/Lexicon.cfm? strongs=G3063>

3. Blue Letter Bible. "Dictionary and Word Search for *Pharez (Strong's 6557)*." Blue Letter Bible. 1996-2010. 11 Aug 2010. < http://www.blueletterbible.org/lang/lexicon/Lexicon.cfm? strongs=G6557>

4. Blue Letter Bible. "Dictionary and Word Search for *Hezron (Strong's 2696)*." Blue Letter Bible. 1996-2010. 11 Aug 2010. < http://www.blueletterbible.org/lang/lexicon/Lexicon.cfm? strongs=G2696>

5. Blue Letter Bible. "Dictionary and Word Search for *Carmi (Strong's 3756)*." Blue Letter Bible. 1996-2010. 11 Aug 2010. < http://www.blueletterbible.org/lang/lexicon/Lexicon.cfm? strongs=G3756>

6. Blue Letter Bible. "Dictionary and Word Search for *Hur (Strong's 2354)*." Blue Letter Bible. 1996-2010. 11 Aug 2010. < http://www.blueletterbible.org/lang/lexicon/Lexicon.cfm? strongs=G2354>

7. Blue Letter Bible. "Dictionary and Word Search for *Shobal (Strong's 7732)*." Blue Letter Bible. 1996-2010. 11 Aug 2010. < http://www.blueletterbible.org/lang/lexicon/Lexicon.cfm? strongs=G7732>

Chapter Six

BREAKING OPEN
THE FOUNTAIN
OF YOUR DEEP

But because My servant Caleb has a different spirit and follows Me
wholeheartedly, I will bring him into the land he went to, and his descendants
will inherit it (Numbers 14:24 NIV).

"All right, I want everyone to try praying as strong as you can, and let's put some energy behind our prayers," was the instruction I gave in the beginning days of our newly formed church. What happened next was not what I expected. The few faithful that came to this midweek prayer meeting looked at me as if I was speaking in a foreign language. Most of them just stared at me with a blank face and an unsure look. I thought maybe they didn't understand what I said, so I said it again. I got the same response the second time, except for a few nervous sounding, muttering whispers of speaking in tongues. They sounded like a quiet helicopter spinning fast out of control in the distance. *So much for strong, intense prayer,* I thought. It was obvious that I had a different spirit than these I was trying to train and develop into prayer warriors who could break through. I could have given up at that moment, but I realized that if I was going to have a strong church in Omaha with strong people, I would need to teach them how to break through in prayer. Thank God I stayed with it even after it looked as though some wanted to quit, but they trusted the Word of God that I showed them concerning prayer.

Today, not only do I have a strong prayer team of intercessors, but the people in my church also know how to lift the roof off and break through in prayer. They pray with such a roar in the spirit and with tremendous intensity. It wasn't that they didn't want to pray strong that day I first instructed them; it was that I had to teach them and impart that breaker spirit that was different than they had experienced or been taught before. I wanted them to possess a breakthrough spirit and learn how to break open the fountain of their deep.

Possessing the Breakthrough Spirit

This different spirit of a warrior and barrier breaker was exactly what Caleb had. We see in Numbers 14:24 that Caleb possessed a different spirit. The spirit that he and Joshua had was a breakthrough spirit that was ready to rise up to the challenge that God asked of them. The only difference was that the people refused to possess the same spirit they had, so they were not able to enter into the Promised Land, except for Caleb and Joshua.

Some people are often like the children of Israel in that they never achieve their breakthrough or develop into a barrier breaker. It is either because they have never been taught or they just refuse to try. Why did God reward such a man as Caleb? What was this different spirit that he had, and how did he obtain it? To answer these questions, it is helpful to look at who Caleb was related to. We have already seen how family ties can tell a lot about a person. One thing that was for sure was that Caleb had the spirit God was looking for. He possessed the same spirit of those we have read about in previous chapters of this book who were determined to have a breakthrough.

There was something in his genes, in his family line, that helped him to be a barrier breaker who had a different spirit. Caleb was able, willing, and ready to go and take what was rightfully his! To do this, he had to be willing to stand for God and stand alone before the people and obey the Lord's will. Does this sound familiar? If it sounds a lot like Jacob the heel grabber and Pharez the child who broke through, it is because they are all related. You see, Caleb received his barrier-breaker spirit and developed it because he came from the same lineage of those who possessed this spirit. Caleb was chosen by Moses to represent the tribe of Judah in spying out the Promised Land. That is no surprise, because we know what the tribe of Judah represented. Judah was the tribe who foreran in praise. In the same way that we are chosen to represent Jesus, who is the Lion of the tribe of Judah in Heaven and also of the earthly lineage of Judah, Caleb also represented the tribe of Judah because of his warrior spirit that saw a big God doing big things.

What did Caleb do that caused him to be a barrier breaker with a different spirit? The most important thing about Caleb was that he was a true worshipper and dedicated follower of the Lord. Numbers 14:24 says, *"But My servant Caleb, because he had another spirit with him, and hath followed Me fully...."*

When others saw giants in the land of promise, Caleb saw victory. He was willing to believe what God said and go fight for it. This is the true spirit of a barrier breaker. They are first and foremost sold out to God. They don't focus on how big the barrier or problem is but rather how big God is and His promise to help us overcome. They stand on God's Word and aren't afraid to step out in what God has said.

I want you to be encouraged because we can all have a different spirit like Caleb and all the family line of barrier breakers. This different spirit is not only speaking of our spirit, our heart, but also an attitude or mentality that prevails. We possess a different spirit than the world to overcome, and we can possess a different spirit as Christians when we fully understand the power we have been given. This is because, as we have mentioned throughout this book, we have a different spirit when we accept Jesus Christ and even more power when we are filled with His Holy Spirit (see Acts 1:8). Being filled with the Holy Spirit and praying in tongues is a key to building up our breaker spirit. Jude 1:20 says, *"But ye, beloved, building up yourselves on your most holy faith, praying in the Holy Ghost."* It is also a great way to create a breakthrough. This comes as we learn to break open the fountain of our deep.

Breaking Open the Fountain of Your Deep

You might be asking yourself, "What does it mean to break open the fountain of your deep?" The answer is in learning how to develop a stronger breakthrough spirit within you and how to release prayers that break through for you, giving you the results that you desire. When you are filled with the power of the Holy Ghost, you possess a different spirit and one that is equipped for breakthrough. We can see our prayers answered and break forth as we pray in the spirit. It can be compared spiritually speaking to the natural water in the womb that breaks before birth. This is what happened to Rebekah, Tamar, and Mary, who brought forth barrier breakers in Jacob, Pharez, and Jesus in the natural. Their natural waters broke, and they gave birth to their children. Prophetically speaking, this is how we receive our spiritual breakthroughs, by praying in the spirit we break forth like the breaking of natural waters in childbirth. Remember when the Lord broke through like the breaking forth of waters in David's victory against the Philistines, calling the name Baal-perazim, the Lord of the Breakthrough (see 2 Sam. 5:20).

When we spiritually break open the fountain of our deep in prayer, we can experience the breaking forth of the water to birth our spiritual breakthroughs as well. This is why Jesus said rivers of living water would flow out of our belly, which is the place of our deep. He was speaking about the power of the Holy Ghost that would be in us and flow out of us.

> *He that believeth on Me, as the Scripture hath said, out of his belly shall flow rivers of living water. (But this spake He of the Spirit, which they that believe on Him should receive: for the Holy Ghost was not yet given; because that Jesus was not yet glorified.)* (John 7:38-39).

The way you release that power is when you can break open the fountain of your deep. This is speaking of your spirit in prayer, by praying in the spirit. You can understand how this spiritual principle works by looking at a natural principle and event that took place in Noah's day.

In the six hundredth year of Noah's life, in the second month, the seventeenth day of the month, the same day were all the fountains of the great deep broken up, and the windows of heaven were opened (Genesis 7:11).

It was when the fountains of the deep were broken open that then the breakthrough came, resulting in the heavens opening and the waters prevailing on the earth (see verses 18-20,24). This is also what happens when you spiritually begin to pray strong in the spirit from deep within your spirit. The heavens open over your lives and situations, and you experience victory. God prevails in our situations like the waters did in Noah's day. This is why the Bible says the deep (God) calls unto the deep in us. Psalm 42:7 (NASB) says, *"Deep calls to deep at the sound of Your waterfalls; all Your breakers and Your waves have rolled over me."* It is calling out to the breaker spirit within us to reach back to God and be released to flood the earth with His power and glory.

This is why it is important to pray in tongues often so we can experience God prevailing for us and through us. This is why the apostle Paul said he prayed in tongues more than others. He discovered the benefits and power available to win great spiritual victories. Praying in the spirit helps to make you spiritually stronger because a barrier breaker is made from within and learns to break through in spiritual realms of conflict. The power to break through is available to us through the power of the Holy Spirit, who enables us to break any barrier we may be facing. Breaking open the fountain of our deep is also how we as barrier breakers can tap into the Holy Spirit's power. This power is inside of Christians to raise up a standard against the devil and win in the battles of life. This is why the Scripture says when the devil tries to come up against you like a flood you can raise up a standard, a barrier against him (see Isa. 59:19). That standard can be the power of the Holy Ghost that is unleashed when you open your mouth to pray in the spirit!

Christians possess this different spirit like Caleb and Joshua had naturally. You gain it spiritually once born again, and you receive power when you are filled with Holy Spirit. Remember that we receive two separate experiences with the Holy Spirit upon our salvation and the infilling of the Holy Spirit. Jesus said in us is a well of salvation that springs up into eternal life (see John 4). This is the first experience upon salvation and referring to the Holy Spirit coming to cause your spirit to be born again. Yet, there is another experience once you are saved that is available. It is what Jesus referred to as the rivers of living water. This is in reference to being baptized in the Holy Spirit with the evidence of speaking in other tongues (see John 7:38-39).

When you are filled with the Holy Spirit, you receive that power in you to break through and become a barrier breaker. As we pray in the spirit, we spiritually fill or build ourselves up. It helps to equip us and ready us for life challenges and gives the ability to experience victory. If you are looking for breakthrough in your life and want to break open the fountain of your deep, there is a prayer in the back of this book to help you to be filled with the Holy Spirit and receive your heavenly prayer language. If you are already filled with the Holy Spirit and speak in tongues, then I want to take you deeper as you break open the fountain of your deep by praying in the spirit.

The Bible tells us that there are different kinds of tongues or diversities of tongues (see 1 Cor. 12:28). We experience this once we break open the depths of our spirit by praying often and continually and building intensely in tongues. We begin to see the different flows and rivers, meaning depths of the Holy Spirit's power. When we develop this in our lives, we enter into the deeper things of the spirit. When we pray in the spirit, we have greater access to the spirit, becoming sensitive to the spirit and entering into the spiritual realm.

> For he that speaketh in an unknown tongue speaketh not unto men, but unto God: for no man understandeth Him; howbeit in the spirit he speaketh mysteries (1 Corinthians 14:2).

There are different diversities and dimensions to praying in tongues, and it is not based on natural age.

- *Stammering lips.* This is usually the starting point, not the endpoint or the continued way we are to pray. *"For with stammering lips and another tongue will He speak to this people"* (Isa. 28:11). This is usually how your tongues sound when you are first filled with Holy Spirit. Your prayer language may sound like a few syllables or childish. We all have to grow naturally and also spiritually, and praying in the spirit is no exception when it comes to the need for development. We grow in our prayer language the more we pray in the spirit.

- *Tongues as a language defined.* This comes the more you pray in the spirit. These tongues may be diverse or different, meaning the tongues may sound different than someone else's, or even the last time you prayed in them. These utterances may be more developed or pronounced, as either the tongue of men or of angels (see 1 Cor. 13:1). This is entering into another dimension of tongues where it is like what happened on the day of Pentecost. They spoke in clear and loud expressions of the Holy Spirit (see Acts 2:4 AMP). Notice "expressions" is plural, meaning there is more than one expression. Sometimes we get stuck in the rut when we pray in tongues and we never have any diversity or ever enter into new dimensions. On Pentecost, the diverse expressions were a picture of them breaking open their deep and releasing well-pronounced supernatural utterance by the Spirit of God. This doesn't imply your lips will never stammer, but you just have to keep developing your spirit and spiritual language.

- *Diversities of tongues and groans in the spirit.* This is where your languages become stronger, more expressive, and unique sounding and more powerful in their operation. It could be strong groaning, different languages, expressions, and sounds usually in strong intercession. Romans 8:26 says, *"Likewise the Spirit also helpeth our infirmities: for we know not what we should pray for as we ought: but the Spirit itself maketh intercession for us with groanings which cannot be uttered."* These are tongues of intercession where you may experience spiritual warfare and strong intercession in this dimension. The result may be unusual, supernatural, spiritual utterances and groans in and by the Holy Spirit.

- *Singing in tongues.* This is praying, interceding, and worshiping in tongues. It is making melody and new songs in your spirit as you prophesize, pray, worship, and sing in tongues. Notice when the believers were filled with the Holy Spirit and spoke in tongues, they also magnified God. *"For they heard them speak with tongues and magnify God"* (Acts 10:46). We also find Peter explaining what was happening on that day regarding the baptism of the Holy Ghost and speaking in tongues (see Acts 2:17-18). He also quoted a passage from Psalms in relation to worship but was using this verse in explaining this spiritual outpouring. Peter, in referring to speaking in tongues, says that our tongue is being glad. Acts 2:26 says, *"Therefore did my heart rejoice and my tongue was glad...."* What did he mean? He is prophesying about the time when our tongue will be glad. We know that he is quoting a passage from the Book of Psalms. *"Therefore my heart is glad, and my glory rejoiceth..."* (Ps. 16:9). In other words, David is making a reference to worshiping God. We can do the same by praying and singing in the spirit as well. This is what Paul referenced in First Corinthians: *"What is it then? I will pray with the spirit, and I will pray with the understanding also: I will sing with the spirit, and I will sing with the understanding also"* (1 Cor. 14:15).

Breaking open the fountain of your deep requires that your spirit, soul, and body all work together to pray strong. It isn't just praying without putting much heart or body movement behind it. Now, I am not suggesting loudness necessarily as much as I am intensity. The reason some never develop a different spirit that is strong and different than many casual Christians is because they go about their spiritual walk and life of prayer half-hearted or very rarely praying, if it all. Those who do manage to pray must tap into a stronger, deeper, more intense life of praying in the spirit. There are two ways that we can further develop our breaker spirit by praying in the spirit. It comes by praying in the tongues of edification and the tongues of intercession. What's the difference? When you pray in tongues of edification, it builds you up. Jude 1:20 says, *"But ye, beloved, building up yourselves on your most holy faith, praying in the Holy Ghost."*

It can be strong and intense but often just for the purpose of personal growth and spiritual strength. This is why people can go to corporate prayer meetings and everyone prays in tongues. Then afterward, they all walk out feeling good, refreshed, and strong. Yet, nothing much changes in the atmosphere or in the things they were praying and interceding for. This is because often they spent the prayer time building themselves up and rarely shifting into the depths of tongues of intercession according to Romans 8:26. To get over into this dimension requires intense, focused, dedicated prayer in tongues, including spirit, soul, and body. It carries an attitude that has come to accomplish something. This is the difference between many who just build themselves up versus those who build themselves up and intercede in tongues. It is like a car that has a standard transmission that requires a stick shift and a clutch. You have to work the gears and the pedal. You have to shift gears and work the clutch. You can't go around in neutral or first gear spiritually speaking, or you won't go very far. You have to be able to know how and when to shift into higher gears. The same is true in praying in deeper levels of the spirit that breaks through for others and yourself.

When you learn the power of developing this breaker spirit like Caleb did, you will prevail over the enemy like he did and receive the promises of God that you believe for. You have to break open so you can break through against the enemy.

This happened with Gideon in Judges 7. He told his men the strategy that God gave him to surround the enemy. He told them to blow their trumpets in one hand and break their pitchers or lamps they were holding in the other hand (see verses 16-20). This took an incredible breakthrough spirit and faith for 300 men to surround several 100,000 men to attack them with a trumpet and a pitcher.

> *And the three companies blew the trumpets, and brake the pitchers, and held the lamps in their left hands, and the trumpets in their right hands to blow withal: and they cried, The sword of the LORD, and of Gideon. And they stood every man in his place round about the camp; and all the host ran, and cried, and fled* (Judges 7:20-21).

These 300 barrier breakers passed the test earlier because among thousands of others they stood out. They stood out differently than the others who were originally part of Gideon's army because they never took their eyes off the enemy. They passed when Gideon tested them by raising their one hand to their mouth to drink, while they kept their eyes on the enemy who was camped out. You probably know the story. They definitely had the spirit of a barrier breaker!

When this tiny army of 300 arrived in battle, they released what God was waiting for. They released a sound! When God heard their sound of faith and saw them break their lamps, the enemy ran in terror!

This represents prophetically to us today a picture of the believer and the Church. We are called to break open the fountain of our deep and let God's power and light break through the darkness and prevail against the enemy just like Gideon's men. It will carry a certain sound. This is because we are the light of the world and vessels of light. When you break open the fountain of your deep in prayer, you release light, glory, and power to prevail over the enemy. Your voice in prayer is like the trumpet, and your spirit is like the pitcher containing light and power for victory. Gideon's 300 men definitely had a different spirit than the 23,000 men who bailed on them in fear or the other 10,000 men who were disqualified by God, leaving only the 300 warriors. One thing is for sure: they were barrier breakers, and as a result of this, with Gideon and his 300, God rose up to their defense and annihilated the enemy. God also showed that He is the Breaker, as the enemy started to kill each other in fear (see verse 22).

The way Gideon and his men obeyed God and put the trumpet to their mouths and broke open their pitchers is the same way we must approach prayer for breakthrough. Gideon's men broke their pitchers open, releasing a sound and light from their pitchers. We do this in the same way spiritually by praying in the spirit. We release a sound in the realm of the spirit and break open the fountain of our spirit, which releases the glory and power to break through. The key is that we pray in such a way that we can break through.

Prayer for Breakthrough

Prayer, especially praying in the spirit, is necessary for breakthrough. I remember recently when I was praying in the spirit in my favorite chair in my prayer room. The Lord spoke a word to me that got my attention. What He said to me about praying in the spirit affects both the natural and spiritual realm. The Lord spoke a phrase. He said, "The tongues of men and of angels." I remembered reading this verse in the Bible but didn't understand how this Scripture applied to praying in the spirit. *"Though I speak with the tongues of men and of angels..."* (I Cor. 13:I). What the Lord was trying to show me was a principle that aids us in breakthrough. It helps us get answers to prayers that bring results. He then went on to say, "When you pray in tongues, you move men and angels!" *How is this so?* I thought. Then I realized when we pray in tongues we move men in the sense that they represent things in the natural. When we pray in tongues, speaking mysteries unto God, we move men here in the earth either out of the way of interfering in our breakthroughs or move them to help us in receiving one.

When we pray in tongues, we also move things in the spirit realm, like angels or spirit beings that either resist or help us in receiving our breakthroughs as well. So, we can say, praying in the spirit will move things in both the natural and spiritual realm on our behalf! It helps us to receive favor both with God and man.

This is what the story of the widow and the unjust judge represents. It represented a widow on earth who needed a breakthrough but was being resisted by an unjust judge.

> *And he spake a parable unto them to this end, that men ought always to pray, and not to faint; saying, There was in a city a judge, which feared not God, neither regarded man: and there was a widow in that city; and she came unto him, saying, Avenge me of mine adversary. And he would not for a while: but afterward he said within himself, Though I fear not God, nor regard man; yet because this widow troubleth me, I will avenge her, lest by her continual coming she weary me. And the Lord said, Hear what the unjust judge saith. And shall not God avenge His own elect, which cry day and night unto Him, though He bear long with them? I tell you that He will avenge them speedily. Nevertheless when the Son of man cometh, shall He find faith on the earth?* (Luke 18:1-8)

We have people like this judge here on earth who often stand in the way of our breakthroughs like with this widow. Yet, this judge, the Bible says, didn't regard God or man. This is a description of what demon powers or principalities do when they stand in a place of resistance over our prayers. This is what happened in the days of Daniel when the first day he prayed the Bible says the Lord heard his prayers and sent an angel for his word.

> *Then said he unto me, Fear not, Daniel: for from the first day that thou didst set thine heart to understand, and to chasten thyself before thy God, thy words were heard, and I am come for thy words. But the prince of the kingdom of Persia withstood me one and twenty days: but, lo, Michael, one of the chief princes, came to help me; and I remained there with the kings of Persia* (Daniel 10:12-13).

There was an unjust judge in the sense of a demon spirit called the prince of Persia that resisted Daniel like this widow in Luke 18. It was the persistence of Daniel to fast and seek God that led to his breakthrough moment. It was also the same way with this widow woman. She put her foot down and drew a line in the sand, not taking no for an answer. She was a barrier breaker who wouldn't give up!

When it comes to intense prayer and not giving up like this widow woman or Daniel, let's look at different words and expressions that often happen as we break open the fountain of our deep in prayer.

- *Travailing prayer.* This is strong prayer that often feels and is equated to natural childbirth. It comes also by praying in the spirit and sometimes with spiritual groaning or weeping. It can often carry the heart and burden of God, and we feel this burden until we pray it out. When we yield to it by the Holy Spirit, we birth our breakthrough moment, bringing it to pass. *"My little children, of whom I travail in birth again until Christ is formed in you"* (Gal. 4:19).

- *Wrestling in the spirit.* This is when you may feel resistance in the spirit against demonic forces, often called spiritual warfare (see

Eph. 6:12). It can also be where we seek God intensely over an answer we desire in prayer. It requires continued intercession in the spirit until we feel a release or sense of breakthrough. While we might not see the natural results, we know a break has taken place in the spirit that will manifest in the natural realm. This is what happened with Jacob when he wrestled for his blessing (see Gen. 32:24).

- *Pour out.* These are heartfelt and unrehearsed sounding prayers that are also part of breaking open the fountain of our deep. They are requests, desires that are deep in our hearts that we want and need to break through in. This is what Hannah did after she was barren. She poured her heart out to the Lord and received of Him. "...*I have...poured out my soul before the Lord*" (1 Sam. 1:15). Now these are not prayers of squalling, bawling, or complaining in unbelief or feeling sorry for self. Instead, they are prayers that pour forth the prayer of the spirit and are often accompanied by the ability to deeply identify with the feeling of need, whether it's in regard to yourself or someone else.

- *Crying out and groaning in the spirit.* These are prayers that come by continual seeking and crying out to God as you remind Him of His word concerning your need for breakthrough. This happened when Israel had been in bondage for over 400 years, that their cries came into God's ears: "*Now it happened in the process of time that the king of Egypt died. Then the children of Israel groaned because of the bondage, and they cried out; and their cry came up to God because of the bondage. So God heard their groaning, and God remembered His covenant with Abraham, with Isaac, and with Jacob*" (Exod. 2:23-24 NKJV). We also know that Jesus groaned in the spirit as a type of intercession at the tomb of Lazarus his friend, and as a result, Lazarus was raised from the dead. These groans can and often will come upon you simply by praying in and yielding to the Holy Spirit.

It might be travailing in prayer, wrestling in the spirit, crying out, or groaning in the spirit—these different manifestations often will come during our praying in the spirit. All of them are important, as they aid in helping us to break open the fountain of our deep and get breakthrough results!

Breakthrough Results

We all want to get results in life and prayer. Praying in the spirit helps us to get results and especially develops that different spirit that Caleb and Joshua had. It also draws out that Breaker anointing of Jesus Christ that we receive when we are born again and filled with His Holy Spirit. Praying in the spirit will help you to achieve breakthrough results.

I remember a time when we needed breakthrough results. We needed barrier breakers who possessed a different spirit. We literally had to spiritually break open the fountain of our deep in prayer. We prayed from deep within our spirits with everything we had. It was a matter of life or death, safety or destruction. The Lord intervened in a very potentially dangerous night in the city of Omaha, where I pastor. The evening started off as an ordinary night with a slight chance of thunderstorms. We were conducting our normal midweek prayer service, when things drastically changed. Within moments the skies were filled with dark and ominous clouds. It began to rain extremely hard, with huge hailstones falling from the sky. We continued to pray corporately, when the tornado sirens began to sound. The news was reporting that there were multiple tornados around Omaha, and one was heading right toward our church.

Things were so dark and ominous, and it felt like there was warfare going on in the spirit. I could tell there was more going on in the heavens than just tornados. We allowed for anyone who wanted to go to other places of shelter in the church. Really it was too dangerous for anyone to leave, and one of the safest places in our church building was the auditorium, since it is an interior space. This is where we were praying. Since we couldn't go outside and there was not enough room to shelter everyone in other locations, we just continued to pray in the auditorium.

As we prayed and praised God, the noise of the winds, sirens, and pounding hail on the roof was drowning out our voices, because it was so loud outside. We just kept interceding! I could tell by the deafening noise of this violent storm that some in the church were getting very uncomfortable. I personally felt at times fear trying to speak to me because of the great responsibility for everyone's well-being.

It seemed we couldn't break through the ceiling of opposition, and this storm that seemed to control the atmosphere. It looked like nothing was changing, only getting worse the more intense we were in our calling out to God. We even had live television reports that we put up on the big screens in the church so we could assess and pray against the many tornados that were forming. The more we prayed, the more the tornados seemed to be increasing. It was getting worse, and more tornados were being reported. I had people divided up in the room. Some would prophesy to the big screens, while others were to not look at the screens but just pray in the spirit as strong and intense as they could. Then I had others dedicated to just praising and magnifying God. I kept encouraging the people not to stop and not be moved by what seemed like an apparent defeat and a disaster for the church and for Omaha.

It was so intense, I felt like we were losing ground, when suddenly it felt like we tore through the ceiling of our auditorium. We broke through! It was as if we removed the ceiling from our church spiritually speaking by the intense prayer and praise to God. Something changed, something shifted, and even though it was still intense outside, we all felt a calm and powerful presence of God and His peace flooded our church auditorium. Then immediately, it changed outside, almost in an instant and to the amazement of the meteorologists on television covering the storm. A peace came over the city, and the city was spared!

As we prayed, those tornados didn't hit our church and our city was spared. This shouldn't surprise us, because when Jesus spoke to the storms they came to peace, and He even rebuked His disciples for not dealing with the storm also. They even reported on the news that it was the "perfect storm" for these tornados to have done serious damage! God rendered the storm powerless by the prayers, and praise of His people in our church and throughout the city! Thank God I had taught them how to pray strong and break open the fountain of their deep. I was so thankful I had a room full of barrier breakers that night!

Breakthrough results took place in the days of Noah naturally speaking when the fountains of the deep were broken open. These things that happened in Noah's days can be prophetically applied to us today, spiritually speaking. The heavens opened, but also the waters prevailed!

> And the waters prevailed, and were increased greatly upon the earth; and the ark went upon the face of the waters. And the waters prevailed exceedingly upon the earth; and all the high hills, that were under the whole heaven, were covered. Fifteen cubits upward did the waters prevail; and the mountains were covered ... And the waters prevailed upon the earth an hundred and fifty days (Genesis 7:18-20,24).

This prophetically shows us that when we pray in the spirit and break forth in tongues, we affect the heavens as they open and respond to our need and affect things on the earth as well. Whatever comes out of Heaven prevails over things on the earth! When we look at these verses closely as to what happened naturally in the days of Noah, we can apply them to us, regarding how to prevail spiritually.

Verse 18—*And the waters prevailed, and were increased greatly upon the earth.* The waters prevailed and prevailed, and the results were great increase!

Verse 19—*And the waters prevailed exceedingly upon the earth; and all the high hills, that were under the whole heaven, were covered.* The waters prevailed, and the results were exceeding blessings and the high places, speaking of the demonic high places, were covered!

Verse 20—*Fifteen cubits upward did the waters prevail; and the mountains were covered.* The waters prevailed, and the result is the mountains were covered, which speaks to the mountains or barriers that seem immovable or too large to overcome!

The reason we get breakthrough results by praying in the spirit is because we have the power of the Holy Spirit to break through (see Acts 1:8). Jesus said this same power would be available to the believer. Mark 16:17 says, *"In My name shall they cast out devils; they shall speak with new tongues."* He was preparing them for this new gift of praying in tongues.

This same power of the Holy Spirit transformed Peter into a barrier breaker after denying Jesus. It also was found in Jesus in the garden when He was faced with the greatest pressure and demonic barriers known to humankind. He broke through by prayer. He could do this in prayer because He had a developed life of consistent prayer before the time when He would need a breakthrough. This is also important for us to have, so we aren't scurrying trying to get a breakthrough without having already made a lifestyle of prayer. Jesus showed us a powerful principle to pressing in with prayer. Notice He went a *little further* when He was in His most desperate need of a breakthrough moment.

> *And He went forward a little, and fell on the ground, and prayed that, if it were possible, the hour might pass from Him* (Mark 14:35).

Jesus pressed just a little further and a little more intensely. Then He asked His three closest disciples, Peter, James, and John, to pray with Him. He had worked with them more closely trying to develop them into barrier breakers. It was in His most desperate need of breakthrough prayer, but we find they weren't of much help. Jesus came back after asking them to pray with Him and found them sleeping! Three times He came and asked them to pray with Him. Why did He ask them three times? It was because Jesus was praying in the time of His greatest need and desired those around Him to undergird and provide support. He was counting on them and looking for them to have a different spirit, like Caleb, who we read about at the beginning of this chapter. Jesus was coming to fulfill the prophecy of Genesis 3:15 and put His Kingdom into the hands of these first barrier breakers, who would help establish His Church and Kingdom on earth!

We have to be careful not to fall asleep in prayer like the disciples did in the garden. This is something the devil will use to cause many prayers to go unanswered. It can be to fall asleep literally or a spiritual condition of many who are apathetic and lethargic. We see this powerful truth in Acts 20.

> *And upon the first day of the week, when the disciples came together to break bread, Paul preached unto them, ready to depart on the morrow; and*

continued his speech until midnight. And there were many lights in the upper chamber, where they were gathered together. And there sat in a window a certain young man named Eutychus, being fallen into a deep sleep: and as Paul was long preaching, he sunk down with sleep, and fell down from the third loft, and was taken up dead (Acts 20:7-9).

The Bible says that while Paul was preaching until midnight, a young man named Eutychus was sitting in a window when he fell asleep and plunged to his death, three stories below to the ground. Paul raised him up and restored life unto the young man, raising him from the dead. I think this is a great example of what it means to fall asleep in the spirit too. The story can be a wake-up call, literally for us today, because of the spiritual state and lethargy of many who are the Church. Many have fallen asleep in their prayer lives and walk with God. In many cases, the Church is like these lights in the upper chamber just like we are the light of the world. Some in the Church have fallen from their third-story place in the spirit like this young man and need to be revived again. The third-story loft is important in its comparison to us prophetically because we are seated with Christ in heavenly places. This is the third Heaven and speaks of our spiritual prayer and position as barrier breakers to overcome in the earth.

We can keep our spiritual place in the spirit and avoid falling asleep like Eutychus when we break open the fountain of our deep, causing the heavens to be opened. Praying in the spirit helps us to stay in our spiritual place of authority and not fall asleep, losing our spiritual position like with the example of Eutychus.

Breaking open the fountain of your deep gives you the results you desire and keeps you strong in your spirit. It helps you to develop a different spirit, meaning one that is not asleep, weak, or apathetic. We must not forget that when we pray in tongues on a regular basis and become good stewards regarding what we have received, then we will receive the breakthrough results that we desire.

The apostle Paul instructed the Church to be good stewards concerning the mysteries that we have been entrusted. This applies to us who pray in the spirit because when we pray in tongues, we are speaking mysteries unto God (see 1 Cor. 14:2). Paul goes on to instruct us to be good stewards over the mysteries we have been given. This includes praying in the spirit and speaking mysteries to God.

> *Let a man so account of us, as of the ministers of Christ, and stewards of the mysteries of God. Moreover it is required in stewards, that a man be found faithful* (1 Corinthians 4:1-2).

We become good stewards when we watch over our prayer life in the spirit and don't fall asleep. We must make sure that we continue to pray continually every day and be faithful concerning this gift we have received form God. This is how we can literally *"Pray without ceasing"* (1 Thess. 5:17). It is time to break open the fountain of our deep and get the breakthrough results we desire. If we want results, we must be willing to apply ourselves and work for it. This comes by a life of seeking and inquiring of God.

Inquire of God for Breakthrough

You see, to get breakthrough results and to experience a life of breakthroughs and victory starts and continues as we learn to seek God. It comes by inquiring of Him. This is how David got a breakthrough against the enemy, the Philistines. He inquired of God.

> *And David enquired of the LORD, saying, Shall I go up to the Philistines? wilt Thou deliver them into mine hand? And the LORD said unto David, Go up: for I will doubtless deliver the Philistines into thine hand* (2 Samuel 5:19).

What do I mean by inquiring of the Lord, and how does it relate to breakthrough? In Psalm 27, we see David praying and worshiping the Lord. He was inquiring of the Lord.

One thing I have desired of the LORD, that will I seek: that I may dwell
in the house of the LORD all the days of my life, to behold the beauty of the
LORD, and to inquire in His temple (Psalm 27:4 NKJV).

David wasn't just asking questions in reference to Him inquiring in prayer. He was breaking through! In this verse the Hebrew word for "inquire" is *baqar*. It literally means "to plough," but it also means to "break forth" in the sense of searching and seeking out. This reveals to us that if we want a breakthrough, it is going to come by seeking God. We may have to inquire of God, which will require plowing through spiritual resistance, and we will need a spiritual hunger and pursuit. This comes by a dedicated life of prayer and fellowship with Him.

It also comes by building an altar of prayer. How do we build the altars of our heart in prayer? The first mention of the word altar in Scripture is found in Genesis 8 when Noah established and altar before the Lord.

Then Noah built an altar to the LORD and, taking some of all the clean
animals and clean birds, he sacrificed burnt offerings on it. The LORD
smelled the pleasing aroma... (Genesis 8:20-21 NIV).

This establishing of an altar appeared to be instigated by Noah and reveals to us how we can build an altar in our lives. First, an altar is a place where you meet with God and commune with Him. It is where you establish your own place to meet and be with God. How many people would break through in life if they would daily establish a meeting time and place with Him by an altar of prayer and worship before Him? I believe this is something the Lord is really looking for in our lives today. Second, an altar is a place where you present something. Noah, in this verse, presented clean animals. We need to bring our lives before the Lord, clean and pure. Third, Noah also sacrificed something before the Lord as an act of worship, obedience, and honor to the Lord. All of these things got God's attention, causing him to be pleased.

When it comes to the building of the altars of our heart, as we pursue breakthrough, it helps if we understand the importance of a life of purity and right living. When we are pure as the temple of the Lord, then we are more prepared, positioned, and apt for a spiritual breakthrough. Why is this? It is because spiritual cleansing helps you to have power for breakthrough. This is why building an altar in our life is important to help us live pure before God. Spiritual cleansing through a life of repentance, holiness, purity, integrity, and honor helps to bring breakthrough in our lives. This is what happened when Jesus cleansed the temple in John 2. There was a breakthrough of miracles immediately following as Jesus ministered after the cleansing of the temple.

> *Now when He was in Jerusalem at the passover, in the feast day, many believed in His name, when they saw the miracles which He did* (John 2:23).

This principle of Jesus cleansing the temple and then a breakthrough that followed can be applied to us today. We are the spiritual temple of God, and we are instructed to take care of this temple and keep it holy.

> *Know ye not that ye are the temple of God, and that the Spirit of God dwelleth in you?* (I Corinthians 3:16)

When we do, then we will not only see things put in order in our lives, like when Jesus set things in order as He cleansed the temple, but we will also experience breakthrough results. The cleansing preceded the miracles. The more we seek to live a clean life before the Lord in righteousness, the more we position ourselves for breakthrough!

This is why it is important to keep inquiring of God in our spiritual temples and rebuild the altars in our life. One of the ways we can do this is by getting the dirt out of our well. What do I mean get the dirt out of our well? Spiritually speaking, our well is the fountain of our deep or our spirit. The more earthly, natural, fleshy things that we keep adding and allowing in our lives, the more they will then eventually affect our access and ability to draw out of our spirit the things we need to break through. Allowing spiritual contamination only further stops the flow of God's power and makes it more challenging to break open the fountain of our deep. We see this natural example of this spiritual principle of unstopping the wells by getting rid of the dirt that stopped the well from giving water. This is what Isaac had to do if he was to experience breakthrough and refreshing. He had to unstop the well. He had to break open the ground to break through to get to the waters of refreshing.

> *And Isaac digged again the wells of water, which they had digged in the days of Abraham his father; for the Philistines had stopped them after the death of Abraham: and he called their names after the names by which his father had called them* (Genesis 26:18).

Isaac had to unstop the wells that had been covered with dirt. We stop our wells spiritually as we put more and more things of the world in our spirit. In essence, we fill ourselves with dirt. Some of these things may not be bad but certainly can stop or hinder the power of God in our lives.

I want to encourage you to go ahead and establish today an altar before God and break open the fountain of your deep. This will help to rid in your life anything that might be stopping up or holding your breakthrough back. It's time to break open the fountain of your deep! When you do, you will develop a strong spirit, a different spirit that rises up to fulfill the will of God for your lives like Caleb and Joshua did. You will unleash the breaker spirit that you have received from Jesus by the Holy Ghost. The sky is literally the limit of your breakthrough. Break open the fountain of your deep and watch the heavens open to you and for victory to start flowing in your life!

Chapter Seven

THE HOUSE OF PHAR'EZ
BARRIER-BREAKER CHURCHES AND BELIEVERS

And let thy house be like the house of Pharez, whom Tamar bare unto Judah...
(Ruth 4:12).

"Hank, will you pastor?" said a voice that spoke to me as I was driving home. It was a gentle but firm voice that was so real to me. It was as if someone was speaking inside the car even though it was just me alone. I remember being so shocked by what I heard that I pulled over to the side of the road a few blocks from my home and soon after I heard this voice. I said, "God is that You, and what did You say? If this is You, Lord, then yes, I will pastor." The Lord knew at this time in my life that I was traveling in the ministry. I really didn't want to pastor. Things have changed in my desire after a decade of being a senior pastor, after pioneering our church with my wife and only a very small handful of people. I love traveling and all the great platforms God has given my wife, Brenda, and I, but the thing dearest to our heart is the congregation of the awesome church we pastor here in Omaha.

When we first started our church, it seemed like we were only having limited results in the growth. I knew in my heart God wanted something different than the status quo and the rising trends of seeker-friendly churches with no power. We began to create a new sound, a prophetic sound, in our worship and praise that was different than many people were used to in the area. People would come and visit, looking at us as if we were too extreme. No, I am not talking flesh and out of control. I am talking about passionate, prophetic praise and worship that is heartfelt, spontaneous, and Spirit-led, a sound that doesn't seek to mimic the songs and the sounds of the latest Christian music artist, even though we do sing many of their songs. Yet, what God wanted was for us to create our own unique sound and prophetic expression.

I knew also that God wanted strong prayer that would sound like a roar and lift the spiritual ceiling off the city and create an open Heaven. Oh, my, that was difficult in the early days, because people wanted quiet, reserved prayer with no power! Again, there was the fight to give in and conform to the religious spirits of our territory, but my wife and I and our church wouldn't give in.

Thank God we didn't, because we have a strong, growing church in our city today that contains the power of God, with signs, wonders and miracles, fresh prophetic praise and worship, and God's incredible presence. God has given us many national and international recognized generals of the faith who come and minister in our church and are blessed by what God has done. This is because God wants a house of Pharez, a whole *house* of breakthrough!

I didn't realize at first that God was establishing a breakthrough church, just like all of His churches need to be. He wants our churches to be houses of breakthrough, or we could say "houses of Pharez."

The House of Pharez

God wants His Church to be made up of barrier breakers, and the Church must become, prophetically speaking, a spiritual "house of Pharez." It is because of the natural lineage of barrier breakers that were born from this family and the fact that he represents breakthrough. A house of Pharez is prophetically implying a house of breakthrough! This breakthrough spirit that God wants is also meant for churches and not just for individuals. It speaks prophetically of a breakthrough Church that fulfills the prophecy of serpent crushers and barrier breakers (see Gen. 3:15).

Remember, God was promising to send a Breaker, His Son, Jesus Christ, through a seed. This Breaker would crush the head of the devil even though satan would not know the full mystery that would continue in the Lord's Church! The devil was so confident he would win that he even mocked Jesus by striking Him over the head with a reed through the actions of the Roman soldiers. It was as if the devil was trying to imply that he was the one who would do the crushing of the head and not Jesus. The devil actually thought he was winning and crushing the head of Jesus instead of God crushing his own head like the prophecy said. However, we know that Jesus crushed the devil's head and accomplished the prophecy through an earthly lineage starting with Abraham and continuing through Isaac, Judah, Jacob, Pharez, King David, and eventually to Jesus. It didn't stop there with just them. We have been engrafted also into this lineage of barrier breakers through the spirit of adoption in Jesus Christ. This is because barrier breakers are not just individuals but rather a whole line of people who possess this same spirit of the original prophetic promise in Genesis. God was looking for breakthrough believers and large family to establish His Kingdom and bring forth His Son, the ultimate Breaker. God wants groups of people coming together as houses of Pharez that the devil cannot stop.

The Illegitimate Children and Generation

One of the ways the devil tried to stop the fulfillment of Genesis 3:15 and corrupt the house of Pharez was through a curse of illegitimacy. He used the fact that Pharez was born from Judah and Tamar through sexual relations between a father and his daughter-in-law. Tamar was not married to Judah when she had relations with him, nor did the Levirate law allow a widow to marry her father-in-law. Satan was counting on a curse of illegitimacy, which, according to the law, lasted ten generations, to try to stop any royal seed or influence that could ultimately lead to the destroying of his head.

No one of illegitimate birth shall enter the assembly of the LORD; none of his descendants, even to the tenth generation, shall enter the assembly of the LORD (Deuteronomy 23:2 NASB).

We can see from this verse that it applied to Pharez, who was born from an illegitimate birth. While the law of Moses here that commanded it came years after Pharez, we know that God took the family heritage seriously because the Levirate law was designed to raise up descendants within that family bloodline only through marriage to surviving siblings. This illegitimate birth could now affect future generations and possibly destroy the lineage of barrier breakers and ultimately the birth of Jesus Christ. It helps us see how much the devil was after the seed and wanted to disrupt the bloodline that would produce the Messiah!

Why would this be a factor that applied to Pharez and the earthly lineage of Jesus Christ? It was because Pharez was an illegitimate child, which meant there was a blood line curse for ten generations. This is why Jesus was born from a virgin; because of the curse on the bloodline from Adam, sin passed down to all who would be born in this world.

We must understand the serious possible implications of what it meant to be illegitimate. According to this verse, to be an illegitimate child could be a child born from an adulterous affair, a child born from incest, or a child born from unmarried birth parents. The birth of Pharez would affect ten generations of descendants who couldn't enter into the house of the Lord.

The reference to an illegitimate child not being able to enter in to the house of the Lord was not in reference to them being social outcasts. It was in reference to the uncontaminated bloodline line in Israel that was to produce the Messiah. Many Bible commentaries consider it too mean that they weren't allowed to hold any office in government over the people of God. They were not allowed to do this for ten generations. Yet, God still fulfilled His plan by waiting for ten generations to pass within the same bloodline to then anoint David to be king. This is why we see in the Book of Ruth the prophecy that Pharez will be the house (bloodline), through David also, that God is going to build the Messianic line through.

However, it was before this tenth generation would be fulfilled that Israel began to desire a king. God was waiting for a tenth-generation child, David, who would rise to break this curse and establish a line of kings that would lead to Jesus Christ. But Israel wanted one now! I believe the devil feared this promise and stirred up Israel to desire a king before the right time. Satan thought he would win by throwing off the timing of God and interrupting the process of royal lineage.

Undoubtedly, the devil knew of this ten-generation curse and thought by diverting Israel to select a king, he would interrupt the chances of a royal lineage of kings coming from the bloodline of Judah to crush his head. Having a king at this time was not God's idea, but Israel was determined that they should have a king, just like all the other nations. The devil used this against them, despite it being against God's plan, and got the people to cry out for a king.

In the midst of Israel's demand for a king, Samuel was instructed of the Lord to go get the king for them. But he didn't go looking for one from the house of Judah. Perhaps he knew that the royal line would come from Judah but also knew it wasn't time because the curse was still in effect. I am sure that this prophet Samuel, as well as the devil, was very aware the prophecy about Judah that the scepter to rule would never depart from Judah's hands. *"The sceptre shall not depart from Judah..."* (Gen. 49:10). He was instructed by the Lord to instead go to the tribe of Benjamin to get Saul.

The king God ultimately wanted would come from the house of Judah and lead to the birth of King Jesus. We know this was speaking of David, but God gave Israel what they wanted in the interim and gave them Saul. This curse wasn't quite broken yet, and Saul didn't reign long as king.

The devil was trying to preempt God's plan by getting the people to want a king apart from God's plan, timing, and apart from the house of Judah. He was trying to get the scepter out of Judah's hand. This would have had devastating results if King Saul had succeeded in passing down the throne; then Saul's lineage would have compromised God's plan. However, God always has a plan that benefits us, and He still waits the full ten generations to continue His promise.

Now these are the generations of Pharez: Pharez (1) *begat Hezron* (2), *and Hezron begat Ram* (3), *and Ram begat Amminadab* (4), *and Amminadab begat Nahshon* (5), *and Nahshon begat Salmon* (6), *and Salmon begat Boaz* (7), *and Boaz begat Obed* (8), *and Obed begat Jesse* (9), *and Jesse begat David* (10) (Ruth 4:18-22).

When you count these generations beginning with Pharez born out of wedlock and considered illegitimate, you see that David was the tenth generation from the line of Judah who could now rule and the curse didn't restrict him in doing so. The reason they had to wait until David is because Judah, who would eventually produce kings for the nation of Israel, had sinned. He had produced an illegitimate child in Pharez as the heir to the throne. Therefore, the people of Israel would have to wait for ten generations before a king could come forth. This is why God waited for David after ten generations and now someone of this family line could rule and be established as king. This should encourage all of us that God knows our future beyond what we do. If we trust Him with our lives and future, then He will establish His plan and break through in our lives. Even though there was an attempt to disrupt it, God still outsmarted the devil and established His all-wise plan!

David was chosen as king, and it would be through his throne that Jesus would set up His Kingdom on earth.

...and you will name Him Jesus. He will be very great and will be called the Son of the Most High. The Lord God will give Him the throne of His ancestor David (Luke 1:31-32 NLT).

After Saul became Israel's first king for a short season, God rejected him for his wrongdoing and chose a man after His heart in David. The Lord led Samuel to the house of Jesse from Judah to find this future king and establish the throne that the Lord Jesus would sit upon.

And the LORD said unto Samuel, How long wilt thou mourn for Saul, seeing I have rejected him from reigning over Israel? fill thine horn with oil, and go, I will send thee to Jesse the Bethlehemite: for I have provided Me a king among his sons (1 Samuel 16:1).

God found David, who would represent His Kingdom on Earth after His heart. God really didn't want Israel to have a king like the other nations had, because He wanted to be their king. He wanted the line breakers to rise up who would bring forth the Lord as King in the form of the Messiah.

This example with Pharez being illegitimate with that curse ending with David reveals yet another prophetic picture of we who are barrier breakers in Christ. We may start off like Pharez born as spiritually illegitimate children until we become like David. When we become born again, we become spiritual kings who are a part of the heavenly lineage of Jesus Christ. *"And hath made us kings and priests unto God and His Father; to Him be glory and dominion for ever and ever. Amen"* (Rev. 1:6).

We have been adopted into the family of God through Jesus Christ, even though the devil tried to disrupt this promised lineage by corrupting previous kings. For a time, the devil seemed to gain ground in this curse of illegitimacy. It started to look like he had won. Yet in all this, the devil did not know the mystery that in Jesus Christ, God had His own seed that would come into play. It was by this that God would break this illegitimate curse off all of humankind through the spirit of adoption by and through Jesus Christ! This is available for anyone who accepts Jesus as their Lord and Savior from that curse. From this, the curse is broken, and these are now adopted into the heavenly family with access to God. In the end, it was the devil who was deceived and ultimately lost. God was in the process of raising up a barrier-breaker generation of believers who would break this curse and set up God's Kingdom.

Barrier-Breaker Adoption

This is why we are no longer illegitimate children once we are born again. We become the children of God as His sons or daughters through spiritual adoption. *"He predestined us to be adopted as His sons through Jesus Christ, in accordance with His pleasure and will"* (Eph. 1:5 NIV).

It is before this that we are all illegitimate children born of Adam and Eve. We actually were children from the devil under that curse. We are all God's creation, but this doesn't mean we are all His children. I have heard many people throughout my life say that we are all God's children, speaking of course about all of humankind. I would have to disagree. We are not all God's children, but rather, we are all God's creation. Jesus even pointed this spiritual truth out before the Pharisees. He distinctly and purposely defined the children of God and the children of the devil, even accusing the Pharisees of being the children of the devil.

> *I speak that which I have seen with My Father: and ye do that which ye have seen with your father* (John 8:38).

> *Jesus said unto them, If God were your Father, ye would love Me...* (John 8:42).

> *Ye are of your father the devil, and the lusts of your father ye will do...* (John 8:44).

The devil is no longer our father when we are spiritually adopted by God through the new birth. We then are no longer illegitimate children. Once we are born again, we become sons and daughters of the Lord Most High. This is important to know because before we are born again we are all God's creation and spiritually illegitimate. Then once we are saved through the blood and grace of our Lord Jesus Christ, we then receive a new identity and a new nature. "*Therefore if any man be in Christ, he is a new creature: old things are passed away; behold, all things are become new*" (2 Cor. 5:17).

We are adopted into a heavenly family here on earth; we can even call God our Father. We are not illegitimate children in Christ. We have been adopted by God the Father. When we understand this heavenly adoption, we then recognize that we are one big family with those who have gone before us in Heaven and those who remain here on the earth as Christians. This means we have been adopted into this barrier-breaker lineage, spiritually speaking, through Jesus Christ, and the illegitimate curse is broken from off of our lives.

We also receive a barrier-breaking spirit from Jesus Christ to handle life's challenges. Every individual has a chance to become a part of this heavenly family depending on whether they accept Jesus Christ as their Lord and Savior. God opens His arms and heart to those who truly will come and make Jesus the Lord of their lives. *"Although my father and my mother have forsaken me, yet the Lord will take me up [adopt me as His child]"* (Ps. 27:10 AMP).

This verse should give hope to us all that God is a loving Father who wants to adopt us as His own. We can even learn from Pharez the barrier breaker, even though he was not born in the ideal situation. He was considered an illegitimate child, but God still used his life to produce a lineage of kings because he carried the breaker spirit! God made something powerful out of his life.

Isn't it amazing that God would choose to use an illegitimate boy to be a part of the lineage of Jesus the Christ, and the Savior of the whole world? Pharez's birth also speaks of God's grace and mercy to give us all a fighting chance and a chance for breakthrough even though we were not born in the right circumstances. This means we all need to rise up above what we may be facing or what life has dealt us and be determined to be a barrier breaker who makes a powerful mark for the Lord in the earth. We can't continue to live in defeat and behind the walls of excuses. The truth is that God's entire house, His Church, is made up spiritually speaking of former illegitimate children, and every one of them needed to be adopted by their Heavenly Father into sonship. *"For ye have not received the spirit of bondage again to fear; but ye have received the Spirit of adoption, whereby we cry, Abba, Father"* (Rom. 8:15).

Praise God, this means we are no longer illegitimate children who can't rule or reign with Jesus! We have been given a heavenly seat where we are seated with Him in heavenly places (see Eph. 2:6). We are not illegitimate children without any ability to succeed or any rights. We have been given the power to rule, because we are now kings and priests unto God!

We have been given authority, righteousness, and right standing with God. We are no longer illegitimate children but now kings and priests who can stand before God in this generation. What generation? I am speaking of a prophetic generation of barrier breakers, who have the same power, and spirit available as Jesus when He walked this earth. *Herein is our love made perfect, that we may have boldness in the day of judgment: because as He is, so are we in this world* (1 John 4:17).

We are not restricted from coming to God and reigning with Him as kings. We have been engrafted, and no longer are we spiritually illegitimate. We are the generation of kings with a breakthrough spirit—a different spirit like Joshua and Caleb. We can possess our spiritual inheritance in Christ. We are seated with Christ in heavenly places and joint heirs. We are not illegitimate without any rights! We have fulfilled the promise of Genesis 3:15 through Christ, even though the devil tried to interrupt and to stop it through the ages. Jesus rose from the dead and ascended into Heaven and is seated as King at the right hand of God our Father!

The curse of illegitimacy is broken off of us through Jesus, and we are now the righteousness of God in Christ Jesus (see 2 Cor. 5:21)! When God the Father sees us, He sees us through Jesus Christ. The Bible calls Jesus the Lord our righteousness. *"In His days Judah shall He saved, and Israel shall dwell safely: and this is His name whereby He shall be called, THE LORD OUR RIGHTEOUSNESS"* (Jer. 23:6).

It says that He shall be called this, but watch what happens to us who are born again who are no longer illegitimate. We don't have to wait for ten generations before our King of kings rises to break the curse. Our King has come to break every curse and destroy every yoke of darkness. He is seated King and Lord of all and gave the inheritance of His Kingdom to us also! Our identity has been changed, and God sees us through the blood of Jesus. Notice now what we the Church, this modern house of Pharez who are barrier breakers, are called! The prophet Jeremiah continues to declare it of us. We are now called in Christ Jesus righteous! *"In those days shall Judah be saved, and Jerusalem shall dwell safely: and this is the name wherewith she shall be called, The LORD our righteousness"* (Jer. 33:16).

Now we know that Jesus is God, deity, the Christ, and the Lord our righteousness. He is called the Lord our righteousness. Yet, God the Father sees us as adopted children in the family line of His Son. This means we are truly spiritual kings who have been given rights of inheritance. Because of this, notice what the verse here says. It say *she* shall be called the Lord our righteousness! It is speaking of the Church! God completely receives us and sees us as his sons, just like He sees Jesus. Jesus was the *firstborn* of many brethren. We are born after His seed! *"For whom He did foreknow, He also did predestinate to be conformed to the image of His Son, that He might be the firstborn among many brethren"* (Rom. 8:29).

The Barrier-Breaker Generation

We are the continued generation of barrier breakers that have the curses of life and of illegitimacy broken off of us. This is by and through the death and resurrection of the ultimate King, serpent crusher, and barrier breaker, Jesus Christ. We are the generation now of spiritual kings that make up the spiritual house of Pharez, His Church, and His Kingdom. Today, God is continuing to build a spiritual family. He waited ten generations to establish His Kingdom through David and then waited again to raise up another King generations later, which is the ultimate King Jesus our Lord.

It didn't stop there. He also waited for this King to break every curse and establish a new generation of kings through a heavenly lineage connected to the Heavenly Father! It thrills me to know that we are this generation of barrier breakers! God knew we were born in the world spiritually illegitimate and through salvation we have received the spirit of adoption and are no longer illegitimate but kings. Just as the Lord handpicked David, God also has chosen His Church, this spiritual generation, to reign with Him. We are the generations of kings and priests, royal barrier breakers.

> But ye are a chosen generation, a royal priesthood, an holy nation, a peculiar people; that ye should shew forth the praises of Him who hath called you out of darkness into His marvellous light (I Peter 2:9).

This generation would be a generation of spiritual kings and the fulfillment of Genesis 3:15 as the corporate seed that would crush the devil. We have gone from illegitimate to legitimate kings! God has raised up a new generation of barrier breakers who are the Body of Christ, His Church. Let's look at this generation of barrier breakers.

> *So all the generations from Abraham to David are fourteen generations; and from David until the carrying away into Babylon are fourteen generations; and from the carrying away into Babylon unto Christ are fourteen generations* (Matthew 1:17).

You see a mystery when you count the generations in this verse. They equal 42 generations when you total them. Yet, when you count the individual generations in Matthew 1:1-16, it lists out only 41 generations.

It would seem a mistake. One generation is left out, but who is this missing generation? No, this is not a mistake but a prophetic generation that is this barrier-breaker generation of the spiritual house of Pharez. Notice the previous verse in Matthew 1:16 that give us a clue into the missing number. It says, *"And Jacob begat Joseph the husband of Mary, of whom was born Jesus, who is called Christ."* I want to draw attention to the phrase *"who is called Christ."* This is a reference to us, the corporate Body of Christ. That is because we are one with Christ, who is the Head of the Church, and we are His body, called the Body of Christ. Christ is the 42nd generation that Matthew 1:17 included. While we are not *the* Christ, meaning His deity, we are the generation of Christ His Church, making us then the 42nd barrier-breaker generation.

We may be born illegitimate like Pharez spiritually speaking, but our spiritual new birth in Christ is also like Pharez in that it is a breakthrough moment! When we are born again, we individually and collectively become part of this 42nd breakthrough generation. Jesus established it when He established His spiritual house of Pharez, who was the Church.

The devil wants to make us think that we and the Church are not legitimate. He does this by making us think that we have no ability to produce anything legitimate, especially when it often doesn't look like we are breaking through or succeeding. We must remember we have the Breaker, the Lord Jesus, living inside of us when we are born again. The Lord's Kingdom is greater than any other kingdom, even when the world may reject His Kingdom or make us feel that we don't matter. We must never forget we are legitimate, the Church is legitimate, and we are the prophetic generation to show forth His power!

We are the spiritual house of Pharez, a generation of promise that will finish the work for the Lord and the apparent missing generation of Mathew 1:17. We are this generation of barrier breakers, the corporate serpent crushing, breaker generation that corporately fulfills Genesis 3:15 in Jesus Christ.

The Church is the missing number that equals 42. The number 42 is especially significant in Scripture. Notice a few examples that apply to this barrier-breaker generation of God's breakthrough Church.

Jesus' ministry was for three and a half years, which equals 42 months. This is prophetic for us as a barrier-breaking generation that we need to do what He did in that three-and-a-half-year span of time. Three and a half speaks of a season when we should realistically be able to accomplish certain tasks. He was showing us our responsibility and job description and was foreshadowing what this generation of barrier breakers would look like. They would be walking, talking, and acting just like Him, teaching, preaching the Kingdom, and healing the sick and casting out devils.

Israel made 41 stops in the wilderness. It wasn't until they crossed the Jordan River into their Promised Land that they reached their inheritance. When we step into our kingly inheritance in Christ, we reach our spiritual inheritance like Israel did when they crossed the Jordan. This speaks of our responsibility to break every barrier as each of the stops of Israel had a prophetic significance that represented a barrier they had to overcome if they were to reach their inheritance. We have been given the opportunity to rise up and take what has been rightfully given to us by God. It was the different spirit of Joshua and Caleb. Because of their breakthrough spirit, they were the only ones of the previous generation to be allowed to enter. This is why we who are this prophetic generation of barrier breakers who have been imparted to and given this breakthrough spirit by God and now part of His heavenly lineage of barrier breakers in Christ. We must rise up and enter in to our promise today.

There were 42 helpers to rebuild the walls of Jerusalem in the days of Nehemiah. This speaks prophetically of us too, who are this generation of barrier breakers, that we must rise up and bring restoration and the Kingdom of God to our cities. Spiritually speaking, we need to rebuild the walls of our cities.

The devil fears this spiritual house of Pharez made up of breakthrough believers. This should cause us to shout as we see that we are not an excluded generation. Instead, we were the generation left unmentioned in Matthew 1:17 because we were the generation still to come. We have been handed the scepter of kingship, where we rule with Him. This shows that God approves of you and me, His Church, and that we are now kings given the inheritance of the Kingdom in this generation. We have been given the power to rule to break-through. We are this generation of barrier breakers in Christ!

This is important to remember because God promised a seed that would arise from a woman who would crush the head of the serpent. We have seen throughout this book God's plan to do it. God accomplished this by the corporate seed of Christ that are the serpent crushers today! We have the same spirit of breakthrough as the lineage of barrier breakers given from Jesus Christ and then on to us. We are called now to be this 42nd generation of barrier breakers, spiritually born illegitimate but made legitimate by the blood of Jesus. Now we have become the spiritual house of Pharez, the house of breakthrough that the devil fears will continue to crush his head, by crushing his authority and wicked schemes!

The Twelve Barrier Breakers

God was working His plan of destroying the works of darkness and purchasing the fallen race of humankind by the blood of Jesus. He continued to protect His seed promised from the very moment He prophesied to the devil that He would send this promise. The devil throughout the process thought he was being successful and didn't count on the fact that God was raising up a spiritual house of Pharez. The devil could only seem to gain the upper hand by an apparent illegitimate birth in Pharez but underestimated the power of his breakthrough birth. He never thought that God would figure a plan that would lead to a barrier-breaker generation in Christ that would continue to crush his head for the remainder of the ages.

One of the ways God continued this process was by what we can learn about the first barrier breakers who came out of Jesus Christ. They were the first 12 apostles. They were the first few who laid the foundation and established the Kingdom of God. They were the first seed of this barrier-breaker generation that would fulfill the 42 generations.

When Jesus first commissioned them, He sent them out two by two, which speaks of agreement. In other words, they were coming in line with God's plan to establish this generation of barrier breakers. *"Again, I tell you that if two of you on earth agree about anything you ask for, it will be done for you by My Father in heaven"* (Matt. 18:19 NIV).

Jesus was raising up the first seed and foundation of this barrier-breaker generation of spiritual kings with these first 12 apostles. He was grooming these 12 to be the foundation and pillars of His Church and Kingdom. We can see this further again by examining the meaning of names. The names of the apostles teach us a lot about what they came to establish and impart into us for the future.

Of course, these didn't start out with a barrier-breaking spirit, but the Lord developed them and even changed their names to help them step into a new identity.

But first they had to be willing to take on that new identity. Before we review the key meaning in the names of the 12 apostles, let's look at Jabez, who was willing to take on an identity different from what he was born with. The Bible says that he was born in sorrow and because of this was given the name Jabez. His name in the Hebrew means *Yabes*, which means "to make sorrowful." This is why he prayed the famous prayer to God that we have come to know. First Chronicles 4:9-10, where is famed prayer is recorded, also gives an insight into his life. It says:

> *And Jabez was more honourable than his brethren: and his mother called his name Jabez, saying, Because I bare him with sorrow. And Jabez called on the God of Israel, saying, Oh that Thou wouldest bless me indeed, and enlarge my coast, and that Thine hand might be with me, and that Thou wouldest*

keep me from evil, that it may not grieve me! And God granted him that which he requested.

He was praying to God in spite of his name because he wanted to break through his own mental barriers that came from his birth. We know this because he was asking for God's blessing and increase even though his name was surrounded in sorrow.

This was the same with Pharez and is true for us also, even though we may have been called or referred to as something other than good. Maybe we have been born into something that is not good or honorable, but we shouldn't be discouraged or give up, because we have access to pray to God and become who we really are in Christ. We can experience breakthrough to bring forth something great in our lives and in the lives of others. We need to remember just because we have been given a certain name at birth or called all kinds of unkind things, in the eyes of God we are "the Lord our righteousness." We have been given a name change, because we have been given a new nature.

The same was true for the 12 apostles. They had to be willing to accept a new identity. I can see how Jesus creatively paired them two by two so that their names would not only promote that identity, but also produce barrier breakers.

Look at the names of those who Jesus chose to be the first seed of this barrier breaker generation. Matthew 10:1-4 (AMP) says:

> *AND JESUS summoned to Him His twelve disciples and gave them power and authority over unclean spirits, to drive them out, and to cure all kinds of disease and all kinds of weakness and infirmity. Now these are the names of the twelve apostles (special messengers): first, Simon, who is called **Peter**, and **Andrew** his brother; **James** son of Zebedee, and **John** his brother; **Philip** and **Bartholomew** [Nathaniel]; **Thomas** and **Matthew** the tax collector; **James** son of Alphaeus, and **Thaddaeus** [Judas, not Iscariot];**Simon** the Cananaean, and **Judas Iscariot**, who also betrayed Him.*

- *Peter (Simon)*—He was renamed by Jesus to Peter in the Greek, meaning *Petros*, "a rock." His original name was Simon bar Jonah.

He also represents the Kingdom revelation given him (see Matt. 16). He was paired with Andrew.

- *Andrew (Andreas)*—He is the brother of Peter and former disciple of John the Baptist. His name means "very manly." Andrew (or Andreas) is the Greek word for *man,* that is, *anthropos.*

- *James*—He is the brother of John. His name in the Greek is actually *Iakobos,* or in the Hebrew it is *Yaakob,* which means "heel-catcher or supplanter." This meaning of the names James here in the New Testament is also the same as Jacob in the Old Testament. He was paired with John.

- *John*—The brother of James and one of the "sons of thunder." His name in the Greek means "Yahweh is gracious." So, John is the gracious one. It means that God is gracious.

- *Phillip*—Then we have Philip. Philip or *philippos* in Greek means "a lover of horses." He was also an evangelist (see Acts 21:8). He was connected to Bartholomew.

- *Bartholomew (Nathaniel)*—His real name is Nathanael, but he is also referred to as Bartholomew It is only the gospel of John that records his name as Nathaniel, which means "the gift of God."

- *Matthew*—Matthew is a Greek Romanization of a Hebrew name. The actual Hebrew name for Matthew is Mattathias. Matthew means "the gift of God." He was paired with Thomas.

- *Thomas (Didymus)*—The name Thomas comes from an Aramaic word *teoma,* which means "twins."

- *James*—James again is the same as a wrestler. His pairing was with Simon.

- *Simon*—Simon is called the zealot. Simon means "a reed like grass." It is something very pliable and changeable. Jesus did not change this disciple named Simon like he did Peter.

- *Thaddaeus*—He is also called Jude or Judas. The shorter name for Judah is Jude. Judah means "praise." Jude is one of the half-brothers of Jesus Christ. Judah, the Jews praise or praised one. He worked with Judas.

- *Judas (Iscariot)*—He is the one that betrayed Jesus.

We can see from these names and how Jesus sent them out two by two what we need to do to be barrier breakers and break through. They are also prophetic clues in how we the Church are the spiritual house of Pharez and what we need to do to experience breakthrough in our churches and city. Here is what their pairings together produced:

1. *Peter* and his brother *Andrew*; It is by seeking the Kingdom first and its righteousness, then asking for Kingdom revelation, coupled with maturity, that we will see breakthrough. This reveals that the Kingdom and maturity are essential for breakthrough.

2. *James* son of Zebedee, and his brother *John*; This is the combination of wrestling with God in prayer and against the enemy that brings breakthrough and the importance of grace to break through. We can learn that breakthrough prayer and grace must go together for our victory!

3. *Philip* and *Bartholomew*; We can see from Phillip that he was an evangelist. We need to learn that once we come into the Kingdom and mature. We take our life of prayer and grace and evangelize others, telling them of the Gospel of Jesus Christ. It is a life of witnessing and being a witness coupled with the gifts of God that positions us for breakthrough!

4. *Thomas* and *Matthew* the tax collector; We need the double portion anointing of God and His gifts to break through to reach the world. The double portion of Thomas's name speaks of our inheritance in Christ, and when it is coupled with the gifts of God. With it we will break through and even get the world's attention!

5. *James* son of Alphaeus, and *Thaddaeus*; This is again breakthrough prayer and also remembering that James is a name from the Hebrew name Jacob, which means "heel grabber," and Thaddaeus is another name for Judas, which is where we get the Hebrew name Judah. Then we are positioned to take our rightful

inheritance not as illegitimate but legitimate children and praise God leading to our breakthrough!

6. *Simon* the Zealot and *Judas* Iscariot, who betrayed him; This is the importance of being teachable and changeable like Simon's name and praising God in accordance with the name Judas from the Hebrew name Judah. It reveals to us that a life of zeal and pursuit of God coupled with praise will help us to breakthrough!

We can see from these the kinds of things we need to include for our breakthroughs as well. It is also interesting that eventually the pairs changed; for example, Thomas started with Matthew (see Matt. 10:2) but finished in a pair with Philip (see Acts 1:13). The Bible doesn't say why, but the Holy Spirit always has a reason in changing the way the pairs worked together. I think it has a lot to do to with our spiritual season of growth.

There was another linking together of the disciples by Jesus that reveals the foundation of these barrier breakers. He establishes Peter, James, and John as the three disciples that He is maturing into deeper responsibilities and experiences with Him. It is also interesting to note that David had 30 mighty men, of whom three were the chief captains. They were barrier breakers also, because they broke through the host of the Philistines. They drew water out of the well of Bethlehem, which was by the gate, and took it and brought it to David (see 2 Sam. 23:16). The names of these three men were Adino, Eleazar, and Shammah. This is because the Bible reveals there is power in a threefold cord that can't be easily broken (see Eccles. 4:12).

Jesus often took separately with Him Peter, James, and John. This cord of three strands of Peter, James, and John reveals another pattern for breakthrough that we need in this generation and spiritual houses of Pharez. We need the Kingdom, power, revelation, and keys. This is what Peter stands for. He was the one to whom the keys of the Kingdom revelation were given.

We also need the breakthrough spirit, wrestling in the spirit to advance the Kingdom. That is what James represents. Then finally we do this by the grace of God, that is John. In other words, Peter, James, and John are a prophetic pattern of Kingdom, breakthrough, and grace!

Notice also there were certain events that only these three were allowed to witness or participate in. We need to examine why, so we can see what it was that they carried that allowed them entrance into the deeper things of the spirit.

- *Raising up of Jairus' daughter.* Jesus only allowed these three apostles when He raised Jairus' daughter from the dead (see Mark 5:37). This represents revival, which means life again, to raise up the Church like this man's daughter. We need stability, Kingdom (Peter), wrestling with God and against the devil (James) through the grace of God (John).

- *When Jesus was transfigured.* He took them along when He showed them His glory by being transfigured before them (see Mark 9:1). This shows how to bring the glory of God to our lives and churches. We need the Kingdom (Peter), breakthrough wrestling in prayer (James), and grace (John). This is the same when Jesus taught them how to pray in Luke 11 and in Matthew 6 in the Lord's Prayer. It was another progression for His glory to come when Jesus prayed regarding the Kingdom, power and glory. He said, "*...For thine is the Kingdom, the power and the glory for ever, Amen*" (Matt. 6:13). Notice the progression of the Kingdom: first the power to break through and then the glory that begins to manifest.

- *Concerning private matters and end times.* He told them privately regarding the events of the end times, taking Andrew also (see Mark 13:3). This shows us how we too can receive the Lord's secrets and revelation. When we apply the Kingdom (Peter), breakthrough prayer (James), and stay in grace (John), we will come to maturity (Andrew).

- *Deeper prayer and commitment to pray.* He took these three apart with Him separate from the other disciples in the garden to pray (see Mark 14:33). This shows us how to stay committed in prayer and step into deeper prayer that leads to breakthrough. We need the Kingdom revelation and stability (Peter), which leads to breakthrough by wrestling with God and against the devil (James). When we do this, we release and have grace (John) to submit to God's plans for our lives for breakthrough!

- *In releasing the power of the Holy Spirit to be refreshed and a witness.* These three are mentioned first as the 120 in the upper room, along with Andrew. Acts 1:13 says, "...*Peter, and James, and John, and Andrew, Philip, and Thomas, Bartholomew, and Matthew, James the son of Alphaeus, and Simon Zelotes, and Judas the brother of James.*" This reveals the importance of how to create a breakthrough that releases the Holy Spirit's power for us, to us, and through us! We need Kingdom first (Peter). Continue to pray and wrestle with God against the devil (James). This releases the grace of God that is available (John) to mature (Andrew). It positions us to evangelize (Philip) in true double portion power (Thomas). We do this through the gifts of God (Bartholomew, Matthew). Staying in prayer and grabbing our inheritance (James), as we do this with zeal being bendable, teachable (Simon), and live a life of praise (Judas) to God. The result will be we will help to release the power of the Holy Ghost as barrier breakers as they did!

This is not a coincidence that their names are linked together, prophetically speaking, nor was it by chance that Jesus seemed to develop these three apart from the other disciples. This was a foundation that Jesus was establishing with these three that would be vital later concerning the building of His Kingdom. They were becoming pillars for this new generation of barrier breakers called the Church. Paul even referred to them as pillars to him and the Church as well. "*In fact, James, Peter, and John, who were known as pillars of the church, recognized the gift God had given me*" (Gal. 2:9 NLT).

We can learn from the pattern that Jesus established in how to break through. God is looking for those who will walk in unity and agreement within His Church and fulfill His desire to build His Kingdom and reach the world for Jesus. This is why Jesus established the foundation of the three and also paired His disciples up. We have a choice: we can either obey our flesh or be like Zerah, who wasn't chosen to be the generation that brings forth the Barrier

Breaker, or we can choose to be like Pharez and break through. There are those that will choose to breakthrough and those who will not.

This is why these names being paired together reveal the tools we need to be barrier-breaking believers and breakthrough churches.

The Characteristics of the House of Pharez

We have the spirit and the equipment of what we need to become barrier breakers in this generation. We have been reading throughout this book the characteristics of a barrier breaker and what God is looking for in one. We can see that God wants His Church to become a spiritual house of Pharez locally and universally that has this barrier-breaking spirit.

There are certain traits that help us to identify churches that are true houses of Pharez or breakthrough. It is through these things that the spirit of breakthrough is imparted and released to bring victory for God's people and defeat to the devil.

We become breakthrough churches and believers that make up a spiritual "houses of Pharez." The Book of Ruth tells us of a word spoken to Boaz at the time when he married Ruth that speaks of his house becoming the house of Pharez. We know from this prophetic statement about Pharez that his entire house was to become a "house of one who breaks through!" It is as we read before; even though Pharez was born illegitimate, his birth was a breakthrough, and his life became a life of destiny that led to future generations being blessed. This was not only a prophetic picture of barrier-breaking churches but of the future Church that would be born with the coming Messiah, Jesus Christ.

It is important that each church and believer who has been adopted into God's heavenly family possess the barrier-breaker spirit when they are born again. They should have these characteristics of a spiritual "house of Pharez." God needs these types of churches and barrier-breaking believers who make up this powerful prophetic generation in Christ. *"And let thy house be like the house of Pharez, whom Tamar bare unto Judah..."* (Ruth 4:12).

They have:

- Strong prayer—"A house of prayer not a few of prayer" (see Luke 19:46).

- *Strong breakthrough tongues!*—They know how to break open the fountain of their deep in praying tongues (see Gen. 7, John 7, Acts 4).

- *Strong praise and worship*—They tap into the dimension and realm of high [raise to break through spiritual darkness and open the heavens] (see Ps. 149, Isa. 42, Isa. 30, Luke 19).

- *Strong giving and serving*—They are committed to a life of giving and serving, using it as a seed and weapon to create breakthrough (see Acts 4).

- *Strong evangelism*—They don't just hand out gospel literature, but they teach, preach the Kingdom, and evangelize by casting out demons and healing the sick, demonstrating the Kingdom and its power! (see Mark 16, Luke 10).

- *Strong commitment and serving of the vision*—They are loyal and deeply committed to the local church and God's Kingdom because they understand the power of being in one accord. A spiritual house of clusters that releases the new wine of the Holy Ghost (see Acts 1, 2, 4, 5; Isa. 65:8).

- *Strong engaging of the enemy*—They understand the importance of spiritual intensity and engaging their spiritual enemy. They are strong in prayer that is like a battering ram that breaks through the enemy's barriers and resistance! (see Ezek. 4; 2 Kings 13).

When we include these things in our lives and also our churches, then we become a spiritual house of Pharez that breaks through! We won't just exist in life but break through! We won't let the devil deceive us into thinking we aren't legitimate. Remember, our spiritual birth is a breakthrough moment like Pharez. We have become part of something great! We are adopted into a chosen generation, a royal priesthood, and are born again to be the barrier breakers who will together continue to crush the devil's head. Rise up, barrier breaker!

Take hold of what is rightfully yours as a king! I guarantee you will experience breakthrough after breakthrough. It's your moment to succeed!

ONE VOICE MINISTRIES
THE MINISTRY OF
HANK & BRENDA KUNNEMAN

CONFERENCES

Hank and Brenda travel globally ministering in churches, conferences, and conventions. They bring relevant biblical messages from a prophetic viewpoint, and their dynamic preaching style is coupled with the demonstrations of the Holy Spirit. Though they preach at events separately, they are especially known for their unique platform of ministry together as a team in the ministry of the gifts of the Spirit. For additional information about scheduling a ministry or church conference with Hank and/or Brenda you may contact One Voice Ministries at 402.896.6692 or you may request a ministry packet online at ovm.org

BOOKS, PRODUCTS, AND RESOURCES

Books, audio, and video material are available at the Kunneman's online store at ovm.org. Book titles include, *When Your Life Has Been Tampered With, Don't Leave God Alone, The Supernatural You, The Revealer of Secrets,* and *Hide and Seek, & Chaos in the King's Court.* The One Voice Ministries' website also provides many ministry resources including Hank's page called *Prophetic Perspectives,* providing excerpts and prophetic insight on world events. Brenda's page, *The Daily Prophecy,* is a daily prophetic word which has changed lives around the world. There are also numerous articles for study.

LORD OF HOSTS CHURCH

Hank and Brenda Kunneman also pastor Lord of Hosts Church in Omaha, Nebraska. Combined with sound teaching, captivating praise and worship and a prophetic flair, services at Lord of Hosts Church are always rich with the presence of God. Lord of Hosts Church is known for its solid team of leaders, organized style and ministry that touches the everyday needs of people. Through the many avenues of ministry the church is raising up strong believers. Many ministries globally have referred to Lord of Hosts Church to be among the most up and coming, cutting-edge churches in the United States. Further information about Lord of Hosts Church can be found by calling 402.896.6692 or online at lohchurch.org and ovm.org

PASTORS HANK AND BRENDA KUNNEMAN
LORD OF HOSTS CHURCH & ONE VOICE MINISTRIES
5351 S. 139TH PLAZA | OMAHA, NEBRASKA 68137
PHONE: (402) 896-6692 | FAX: (402) 894-9068
OVM.ORG | LOHCHURCH.ORG

Other Books by Hank Kunneman

Don't Leave God Alone; The Revealer of Secrets

IN THE RIGHT HANDS THIS BOOK WILL CHANGE LIVES!

Most of the people that need this message will not be looking for this book. To change their life you need to put a copy of this book in their hands.

> *But others (seeds) fell into good ground, and brought forth fruit, some a hundred-fold, some sixty-fold, some thirty-fold* (Matthew 13:3-8).

Our ministry is constantly seeking methods to find the good ground, the people that need this anointed message to change their life. Will you help us reach these people?

> *Remember this—a farmer who plants only a few seeds will get a small crop. But the one who plants generously will get a generous crop* (2 Corinthians 9:6).

EXTEND THIS MINISTRY BY SOWING
3-BOOKS, 5-BOOKS, 10-BOOKS, OR MORE TODAY,
AND BECOME A LIFE CHANGER!

Thank you,

Don Nori Sr., Publisher
Destiny Image
Since 1982